THE BIG BOOK OF
CHRISTMAS
QUiCKIES

LEISURE ARTS, INC.
Little Rock, Arkansas

THE BIG BOOK OF CHRISTMAS QUICKIES

EDITORIAL STAFF

Vice President and Editor-in-Chief: Sandra Graham Case
Executive Director of Publications: Cheryl Nodine Gunnells
Director of Designer Relations: Debra Nettles
Publications Director: Susan White Sullivan
Editorial Director: Susan Frantz Wiles
Photography Director: Lori Ringwood Dimond
Art Operations Director: Jeff Curtis

PRODUCTION
Managing Editor: Mary Sullivan Hutcheson
Instructional Editors: Carolyn Breeding and Karen Jackson
Production Assistants: Karla Edgar, Mimi Harrington, and
    Frances Huddleston

EDITORIAL
Managing Editor: Suzie Puckett
Associate Editor: Darla Burdette Kelsay

ART
Senior Art Director: Rhonda Hodge Shelby
Senior Production Artist: Steph Cordero Johnson
Lead Production Artist: Teresa Boyd
Production Artists: Clint Hanson, Chaska Richardson Lucas,
    and John Rose
Color Technician: Mark Hawkins
Photography Stylist: Janna Laughlin
Staff Photographer: Russ Ganser
Publishing Systems Administrator: Becky Riddle
Publishing Systems Assistants: Myra S. Means and
    Chris Wertenberger

BUSINESS STAFF

Publisher: Rick Barton
Vice President, Finance: Tom Siebenmorgen
Director of Corporate Planning and Development:
    Laticia Mull Cornett
Vice President, Retail Marketing: Bob Humphrey
Vice President, Sales: Ray Shelgosh

Vice President, National Accounts: Pam Stebbins
Director of Sales and Services: Margaret Reinold
Vice President, Operations: Jim Dittrich
Comptroller, Operations: Rob Thieme
Retail Customer Service Manager: Wanda Price
Print Production Manager: Fred F. Pruss

Made in the United States of America.
Softcover ISBN 1-57486-256-1

10 9 8 7 6 5 4 3 2 1

OCT 0 8 2002

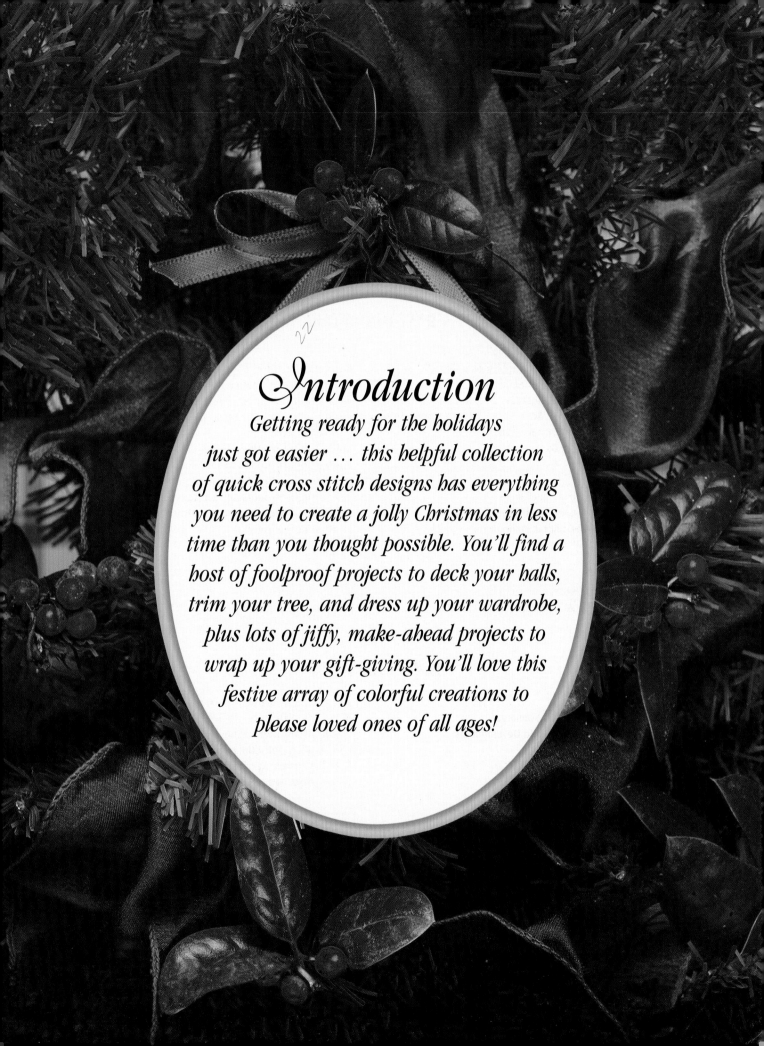

Introduction

*Getting ready for the holidays
just got easier … this helpful collection
of quick cross stitch designs has everything
you need to create a jolly Christmas in less
time than you thought possible. You'll find a
host of foolproof projects to deck your halls,
trim your tree, and dress up your wardrobe,
plus lots of jiffy, make-ahead projects to
wrap up your gift-giving. You'll love this
festive array of colorful creations to
please loved ones of all ages!*

Table

ORNAMENTS FOR EVERYONE

FESTIVE FASHIONS

of Contents

Ornaments for Everyone

One thing we've discovered over the years is that you can never have enough Christmas ornaments! That's why we've packed this section full of quick-to-make projects perfect for trimming trees of every size and style. Why not choose your favorites today? It's never too early to start thinking about Christmas!

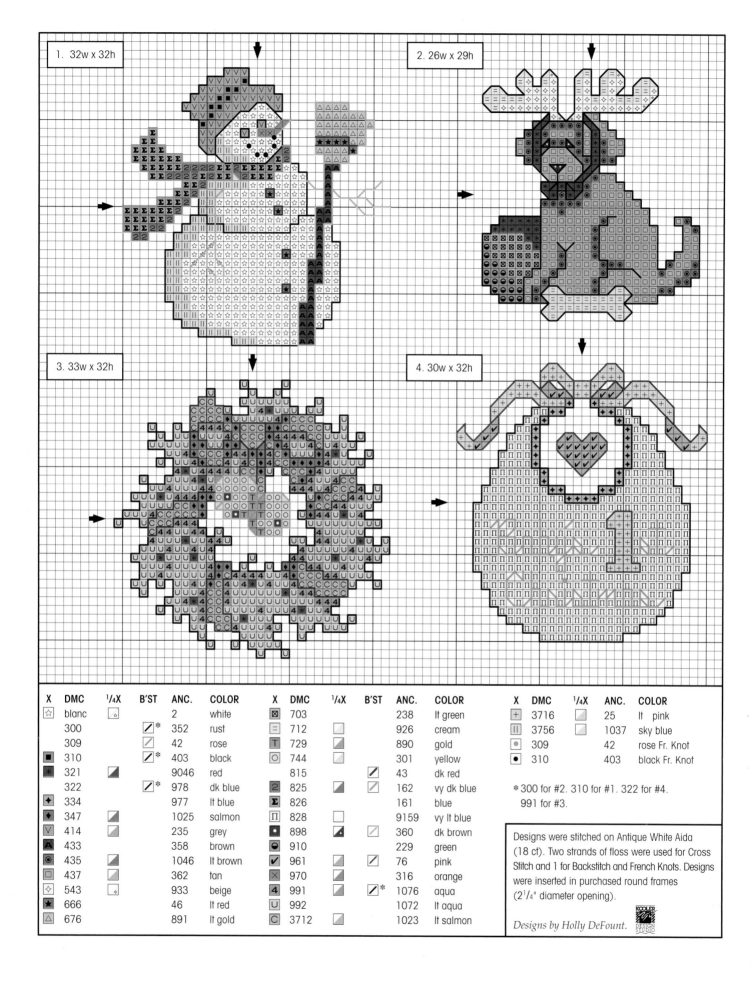

X	DMC	¼X	B'ST	ANC.	COLOR	X	DMC	¼X	B'ST	ANC.	COLOR	X	DMC	¼X	ANC.	COLOR
☆	blanc	⸰		2	white	⊠	703			238	lt green	+	3716		25	lt pink
	300		✒*	352	rust	▤	712	◪		926	cream	‖	3756	◪	1037	sky blue
	309		✒	42	rose	T	729	◪		890	gold	⊙	309		42	rose Fr. Knot
■	310		✒*	403	black	O	744	◪		301	yellow	●	310		403	black Fr. Knot
▧	321	◪		9046	red		815		✒	43	dk red					
	322		✒*	978	dk blue	2	825	◪		162	vy dk blue	*300 for #2. 310 for #1. 322 for #4.				
◆	334			977	lt blue	Σ	826			161	blue	991 for #3.				
◆	347	◪		1025	salmon	Π	828			9159	vy lt blue					
V	414	◪		235	grey	◼	898	◪		360	dk brown					
▲	433			358	brown	◓	910			229	green	Designs were stitched on Antique White Aida				
◉	435	◪		1046	lt brown	✔	961	◪	✒	76	pink	(18 ct). Two strands of floss were used for Cross				
▢	437	◪		362	tan	✕	970			316	orange	Stitch and 1 for Backstitch and French Knots. Designs				
◇	543	⬦		933	beige	4	991	◪	✒*	1076	aqua	were inserted in purchased round frames				
★	666			46	lt red	U	992			1072	lt aqua	(2¼" diameter opening).				
△	676			891	lt gold	C	3712	◪		1023	lt salmon	*Designs by Holly DeFount.*				

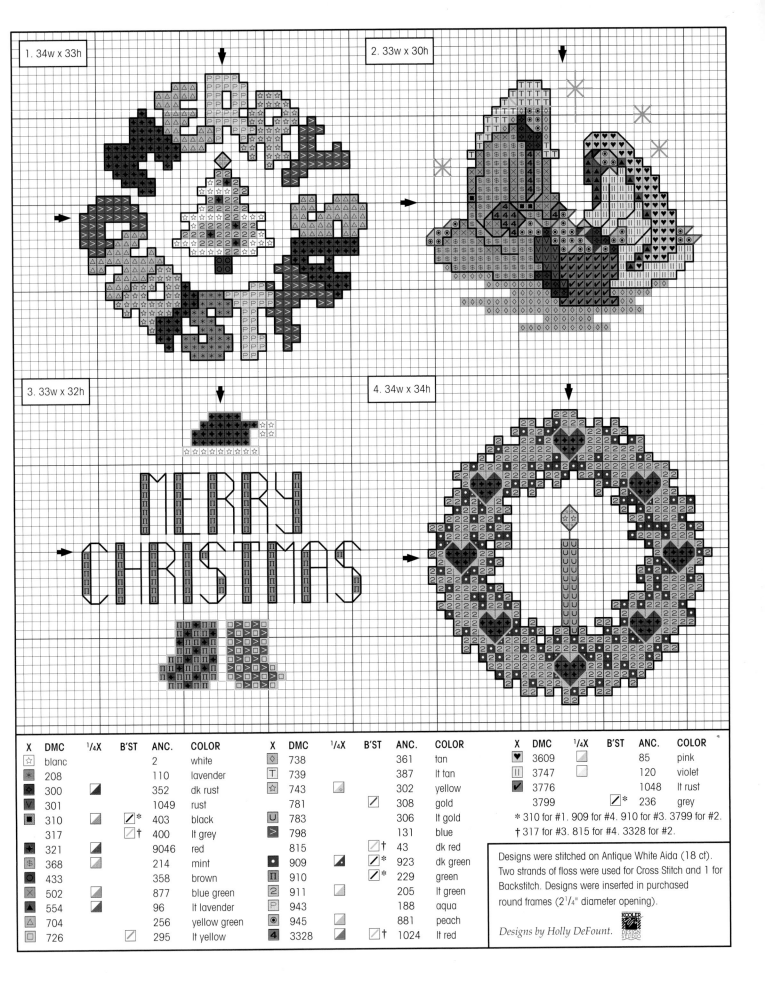

1. 34w x 33h

2. 33w x 30h

3. 33w x 32h

4. 34w x 34h

MERRY CHRISTMAS

X	DMC	1/4X	B'ST	ANC.	COLOR	X	DMC	1/4X	B'ST	ANC.	COLOR	X	DMC	1/4X	B'ST	ANC.	COLOR
☆	blanc			2	white	◇	738			361	tan	♥	3609			85	pink
✳	208			110	lavender	T	739			387	lt tan	‖	3747			120	violet
✦	300	◢		352	dk rust	☆	743	◢		302	yellow	✔	3776			1048	lt rust
V	301			1049	rust		781		◢	308	gold		3799		◢*	236	grey
■	310	◢	◢*	403	black	U	783			306	lt gold						
	317		◢†	400	lt grey	>	798			131	blue	*310 for #1. 909 for #4. 910 for #3. 3799 for #2.
✚	321	◢		9046	red		815		◢†	43	dk red	†317 for #3. 815 for #4. 3328 for #2.
$	368	◢		214	mint	●	909	◢	◢*	923	dk green	
◉	433			358	brown	Π	910		◢*	229	green	Designs were stitched on Antique White Aida (18 ct). Two strands of floss were used for Cross Stitch and 1 for Backstitch. Designs were inserted in purchased round frames (2¼" diameter opening).
×	502	◢		877	blue green	2	911	◢		205	lt green	
▲	554	◢		96	lt lavender	P	943			188	aqua	
△	704			256	yellow green	◉	945	◢		881	peach	*Designs by Holly DeFount.*
▢	726		◢	295	lt yellow	4	3328	◢	◢†	1024	lt red	

9

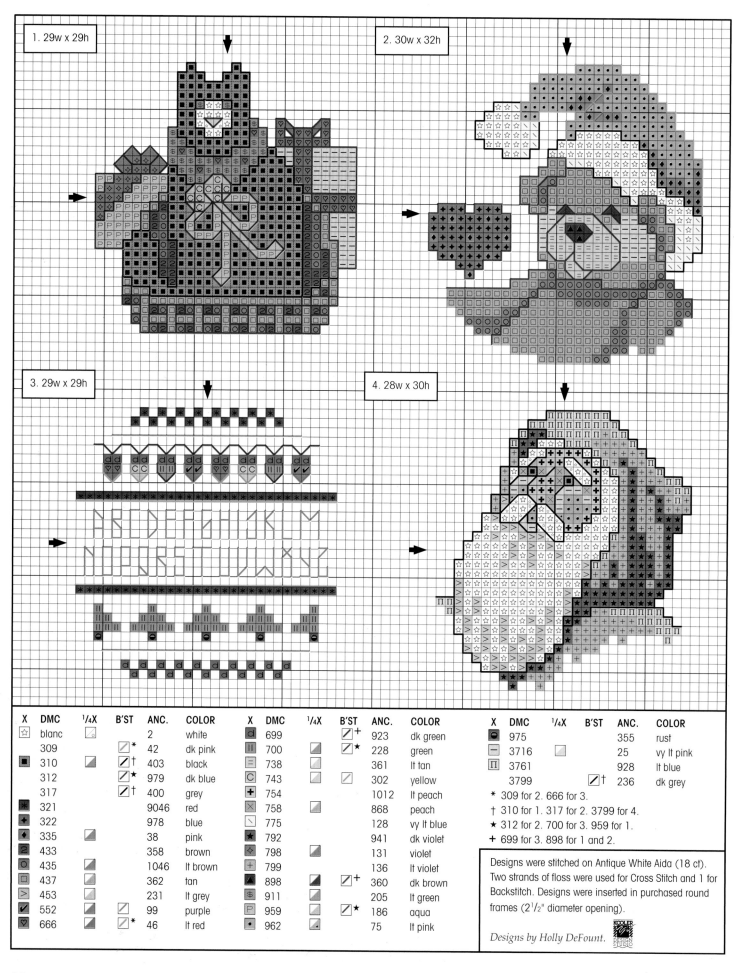

X	DMC	¼X	B'ST	ANC.	COLOR	X	DMC	¼X	B'ST	ANC.	COLOR	X	DMC	¼X	B'ST	ANC.	COLOR
☆	blanc			2	white	◩	699		⊘+	923	dk green	⊖	975			355	rust
	309		⊘*	42	dk pink	‖	700		⊘★	228	green	–	3716			25	vy lt pink
■	310		⊘†	403	black	≡	738			361	lt tan	∏	3761			928	lt blue
	312		⊘★	979	dk blue	C	743		⊘	302	yellow		3799		⊘†	236	dk grey
	317		⊘†	400	grey	+	754			1012	lt peach						
✴	321			9046	red	✕	758			868	peach						
✦	322			978	blue	◣	775			128	vy lt blue						
◆	335			38	pink	★	792			941	dk violet						
②	433			358	brown	◈	798			131	violet						
◎	435			1046	lt brown	+	799			136	lt violet						
▢	437			362	tan	▲	898		⊘+	360	dk brown						
▷	453			231	lt grey	$	911			205	lt green						
✔	552			99	purple	P	959		⊘★	186	aqua						
♡	666		⊘*	46	lt red	•	962			75	lt pink						

* 309 for 2. 666 for 3.
† 310 for 1. 317 for 2. 3799 for 4.
★ 312 for 2. 700 for 3. 959 for 1.
+ 699 for 3. 898 for 1 and 2.

Designs were stitched on Antique White Aida (18 ct). Two strands of floss were used for Cross Stitch and 1 for Backstitch. Designs were inserted in purchased round frames (2½" diameter opening).

Designs by Holly DeFount.

Peppermint Playmates

*Paired with candy cane "sporting gear," three sweet teddy bears make playful tree accents
when stitched as mini pillow ornaments. A carousel cub decorates a dainty gift tote.*

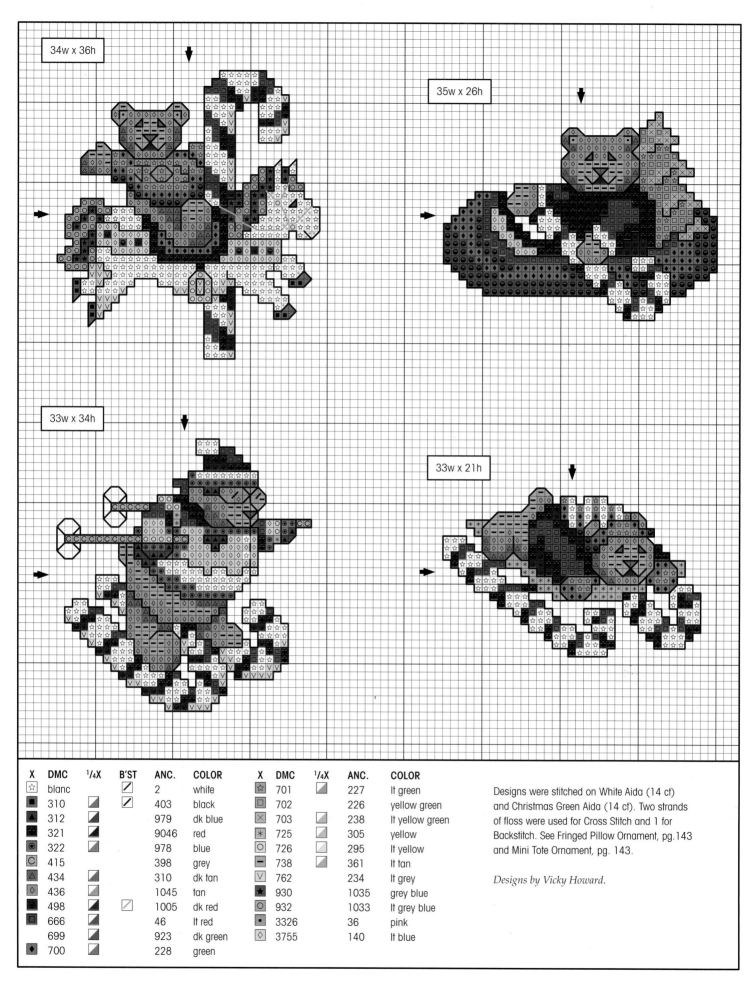

X	DMC	¼X	B'ST	ANC.	COLOR	X	DMC	¼X	ANC.	COLOR
☆	blanc		✓	2	white	☆	701		227	lt green
■	310	◢	✓	403	black	▢	702		226	yellow green
▲	312	◢		979	dk blue	✕	703	◢	238	lt yellow green
■	321	◢		9046	red	✳	725		305	yellow
◉	322	◢		978	blue	○	726		295	lt yellow
C	415			398	grey	−	738	◢	361	lt tan
▲	434	◢		310	dk tan	V	762		234	lt grey
◇	436	◢		1045	tan	✳	930		1035	grey blue
■	498	◢	✓	1005	dk red	◎	932		1033	lt grey blue
▣	666	◢		46	lt red	•	3326		36	pink
	699	◢		923	dk green	◇	3755		140	lt blue
◆	700	◢		228	green					

Designs were stitched on White Aida (14 ct) and Christmas Green Aida (14 ct). Two strands of floss were used for Cross Stitch and 1 for Backstitch. See Fringed Pillow Ornament, pg.143 and Mini Tote Ornament, pg. 143.

Designs by Vicky Howard.

Cinnamon Santa Bags

Stitched in shades of red, blue, or green, our slender Santa really dresses up these simple bag ornaments! To add holiday fragrance to your home, simply fill the bags with cinnamon sticks and place them on your tree and throughout the house.

20w x 88h

Design was stitched on Antique White Aida (14 ct). Two strands of floss were used for Cross Stitch and 1 for Backstitch. See Bag Ornaments, pg. 143.

X	DMC	B'ST	ANC.	COLOR	X	DMC	ANC.	COLOR	
☆	ecru		387	ecru	▢	761	1021	pink	* For blue Santa, use 336.
■*	304		1006	red	○	783	306	gold	For green Santa, use 501.
■	310	╱	403	black	■+	815	43	dk red	† For blue Santa, use 312.
■†	321		9046	lt red	*	822	390	beige	For green Santa, use 502.
V	413		236	grey	△	948	1011	peach	+ For blue Santa, use 823.
									For green Santa, use 500.

13

Christmas Hearts

Ice skaters and a leaping reindeer appear on a trio of heart-shaped tree trimmers. Fashioned with white cord and tassels, these charming ornaments will make ideal stocking stuffers.

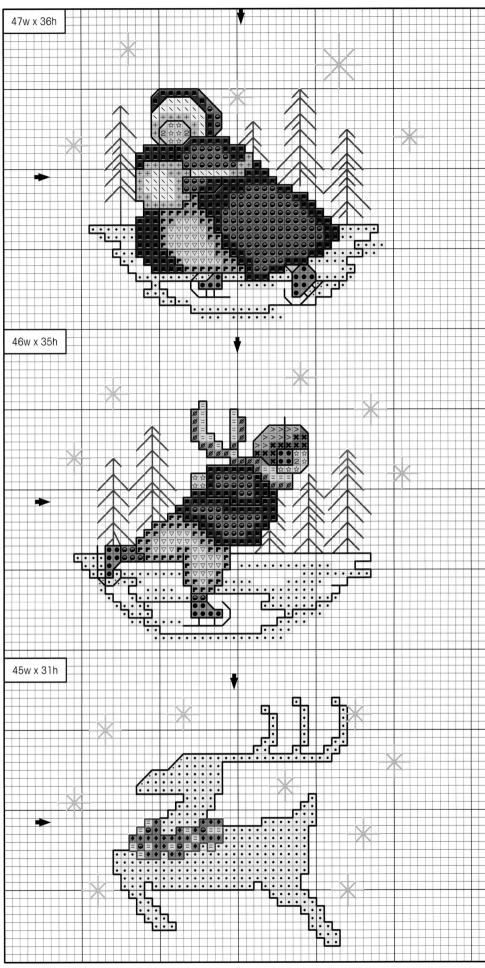

X	DMC	¼X	B'ST	ANC.	COLOR
•*	blanc &	•		2	white
	Kreinik Blending Filament - 032				
↘	blanc			2	white
◕	304	◨		1006	lt red
✕	435	◨		1046	brown
▷	437	◨		362	lt brown
▬	498	◨		1005	red
◆	501		╱	878	dk blue green
⦰	502	◨		877	blue green
=	503			876	lt blue green
⊓	680			901	dk gold
▽	729			890	gold
☆	754	◨		1012	peach
2	760			1022	pink
⬤	825			162	blue
+	927	◨		848	lt blue
	3799		╱	236	grey
			╱†		Kreinik Blending Filament - 032

* Use 2 strands of floss and 1 strand of blending filament.

† Use 2 strands of blending filament.

Each design was stitched on a 6" square of Delft Blue Aida (14 ct). Three strands of floss were used for Cross Stitch and 1 for Backstitch, unless otherwise noted in the color key. They were made into ornaments.

For each ornament, you will need a 6" square of Delft Blue Aida for backing, tracing paper, 10" x 5" piece of adhesive board, 10" x 5" piece of batting, 12" length of ³⁄₁₆" dia. cording with attached seam allowance, 4" length of ³⁄₁₆" dia. cording without seam allowance, and a 2½" tassel.

For pattern, fold tracing paper in half and place fold on dashed line of Heart pattern. Trace pattern onto tracing paper; cut out pattern and press flat. Draw around pattern twice on mounting board and twice on batting; cut out. Remove paper from one piece of mounting board and press one batting piece onto mounting board. Repeat with remaining pieces of mounting board and batting. Center pattern on wrong side of stitched piece; pin pattern in place. Cut stitched piece 1" larger than pattern on all sides. Cut backing fabric the same size as stitched piece.

Clip ³⁄₈" into edge of stitched piece at ½" intervals. Center wrong side of stitched piece over batting on one mounting board piece; fold edges of stitched piece to back of mounting board and glue in place. For ornament back, repeat with backing fabric and remaining mounting board.

Glue cording seam allowance to wrong side of ornament front, beginning at top point of heart. Glue tassel to wrong side of ornament front at bottom of heart.

For hanger, referring to photo for placement, fold a 4" length of cording in half and glue loose ends of cording to wrong side of ornament front. Matching wrong sides, glue ornament front and back together.

Designs by Lorri Birmingham.

Patchwork Pretties

A passion for patchwork inspired these pretty ornaments stitched on perforated plastic. The colorful Christmas motifs make delightful gift tags, too.

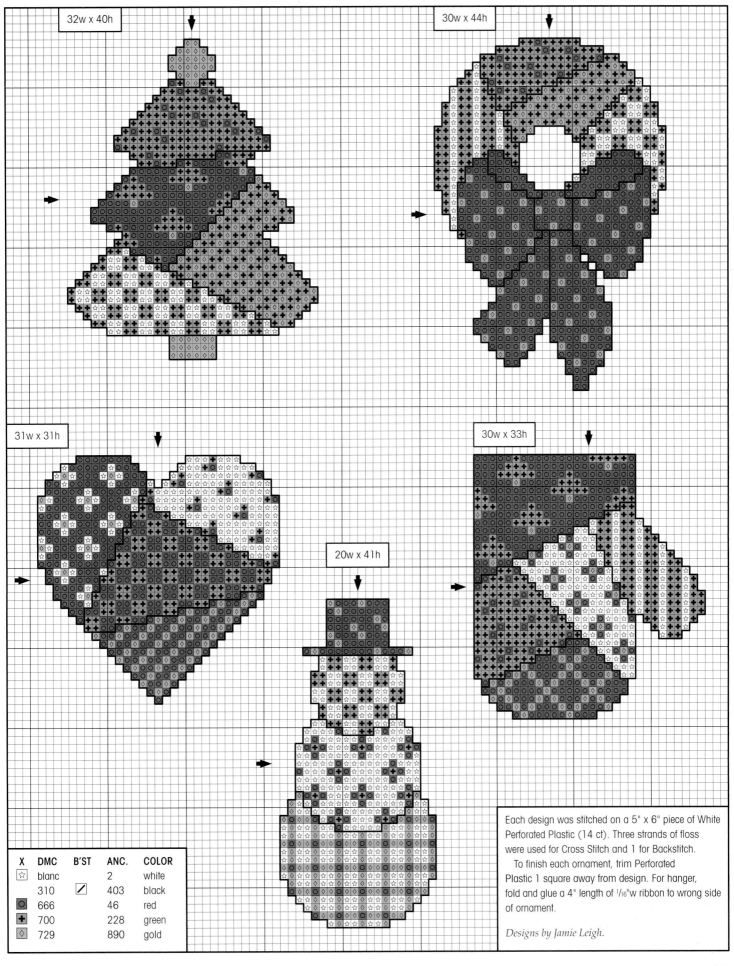

32w x 40h

30w x 44h

31w x 31h

30w x 33h

20w x 41h

X	DMC	B'ST	ANC.	COLOR
☆	blanc		2	white
	310	╱	403	black
◉	666		46	red
✚	700		228	green
◇	729		890	gold

Each design was stitched on a 5" x 6" piece of White Perforated Plastic (14 ct). Three strands of floss were used for Cross Stitch and 1 for Backstitch.

To finish each ornament, trim Perforated Plastic 1 square away from design. For hanger, fold and glue a 4" length of 1/16"w ribbon to wrong side of ornament.

Designs by Jamie Leigh.

Yuletide Trims

*Nothing adds to the tree-trimming tradition
like your very own handmade ornaments. Our
Christmas collection, accented with a few
merry embellishments, will make the branches
of any evergreen a vision of Yuletide delight!*

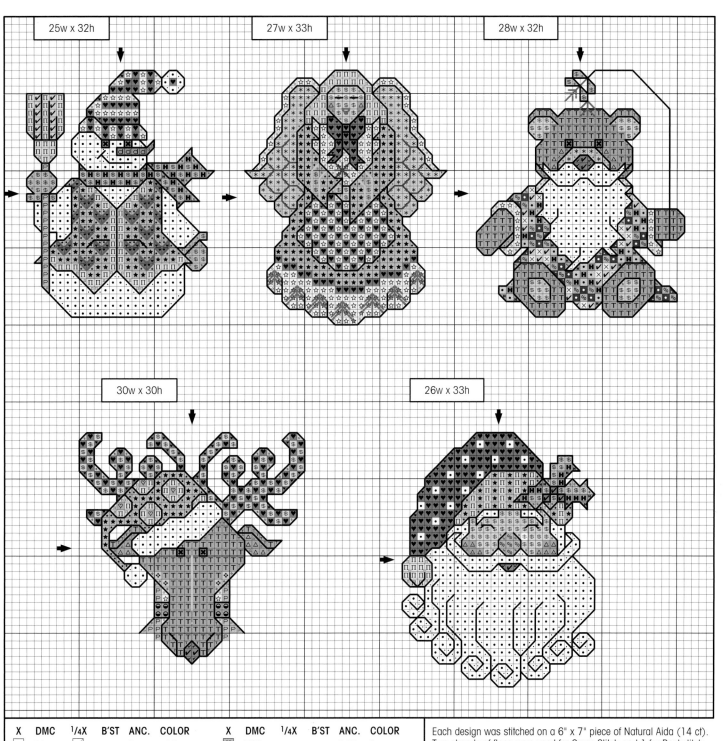

X	DMC	¼X	B'ST	ANC.	COLOR	X	DMC	¼X	B'ST	ANC.	COLOR
•	blanc			2	white	♡	722			323	lt orange
☆	ecru			387	ecru	✕	727			293	lt yellow
◕	320		✓*	215	green	✳	738			361	lt tan
★	334			977	blue	$	754			1012	peach
♥	349		✓*	13	dk red	✔	783		✓†	306	gold
✔	350			11	red	◉	817			13	vy dk red
%	351			10	lt red		822			390	vy lt tan
❖	352			9	vy lt red	✖	898		✓	360	dk brown
△	353			6	pink	Π	3821			305	yellow
H	367		✓*	217	dk green	○	898				dk brown French Knot
$	368			214	lt green						
•	369			1043	vy lt green	* Use 320 for angel's dress, 367 for bear					
P	435		✓†	1046	lt brown	and 349 for all other.					
T	436			1045	tan	† Use 435 for angel's wings and 783 for					
d	721			925	orange	angel's star.					

Each design was stitched on a 6" x 7" piece of Natural Aida (14 ct). Two strands of floss were used for Cross Stitch and 1 for Backstitch and French Knots. Referring to photo for placement, use 3 strands of DMC 367 floss to add scarf fringe to Snowman, 2 strands of DMC 3821 floss to attach 8mm jingle bell to Santa's hat, and 3 strands of DMC 349 floss for bow on bear. They were made into ornaments. See Padded Shape Ornament #1, pg. 143.

For fringe, thread needle with a 6" length of floss. Insert needle from right to wrong side of fabric, leaving 3" of floss on right side; insert needle back through to right side of fabric close to entry point. Remove needle and tie an overhand knot close to fabric; trim ends to ³/₈" from knot.

Designs by Anne Stanton.

Quick Mini Stockings

Send special season's greetings stashed in this whimsical trio of mini stockings. Adorned in bright motifs that complement each holiday wish, these little Yuletide accents are just right for holding tiny Christmas trinkets or trimming the tree.

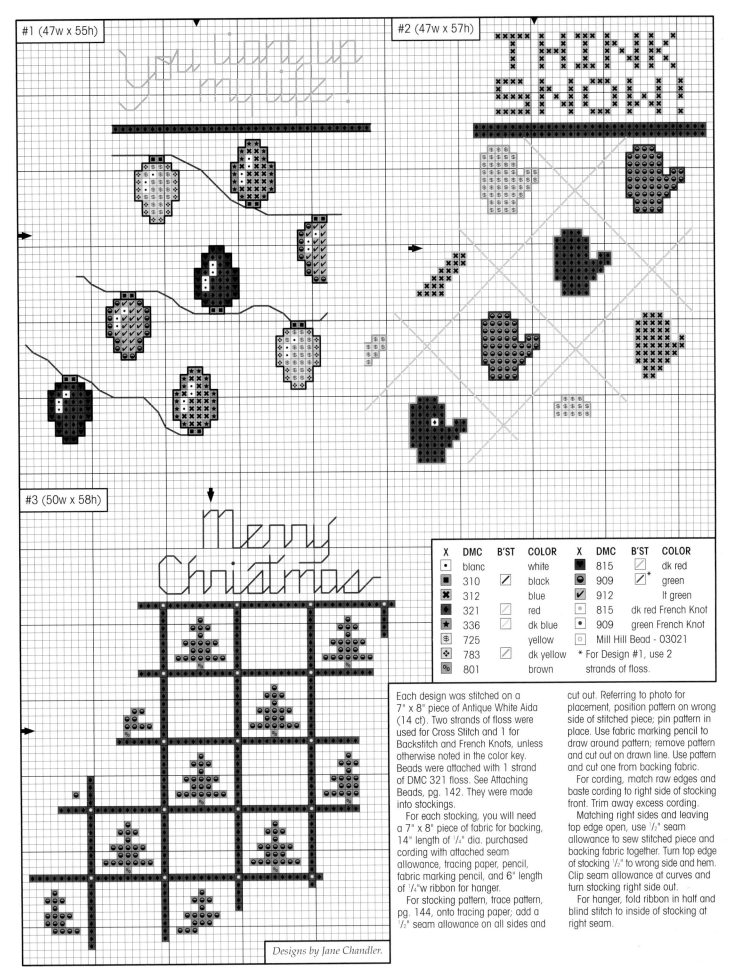

#1 (47w x 55h)

#2 (47w x 57h)

#3 (50w x 58h)

X	DMC	B'ST	COLOR	X	DMC	B'ST	COLOR
•	blanc		white		815		dk red
■	310	/	black		909	/*	green
✖	312		blue	✔	912		lt green
	321		red		815		dk red French Knot
★	336		dk blue	•	909		green French Knot
$	725		yellow	○			Mill Hill Bead - 03021
✿	783	/	dk yellow				* For Design #1, use 2
%	801		brown				strands of floss.

Each design was stitched on a 7" x 8" piece of Antique White Aida (14 ct). Two strands of floss were used for Cross Stitch and 1 for Backstitch and French Knots, unless otherwise noted in the color key. Beads were attached with 1 strand of DMC 321 floss. See Attaching Beads, pg. 142. They were made into stockings.

For each stocking, you will need a 7" x 8" piece of fabric for backing, 14" length of ¹/₄" dia. purchased cording with attached seam allowance, tracing paper, pencil, fabric marking pencil, and 6" length of ¹/₄"w ribbon for hanger.

For stocking pattern, trace pattern, pg. 144, onto tracing paper; add a ¹/₂" seam allowance on all sides and cut out. Referring to photo for placement, position pattern on wrong side of stitched piece; pin pattern in place. Use fabric marking pencil to draw around pattern; remove pattern and cut out on drawn line. Use pattern and cut one from backing fabric.

For cording, match raw edges and baste cording to right side of stocking front. Trim away excess cording.

Matching right sides and leaving top edge open, use ¹/₂" seam allowance to sew stitched piece and backing fabric together. Turn top edge of stocking ¹/₂" to wrong side and hem. Clip seam allowance at curves and turn stocking right side out.

For hanger, fold ribbon in half and blind stitch to inside of stocking at right seam.

Designs by Jane Chandler.

Tiny Tree

A rustic reminder of the season awaits those who make our mini Christmas tree! Created using long stitches on an earthy fabric and twinkling with seed bead "lights," the evergreen looks right at home on this holiday ornament.

The design was stitched on a 7" square of Zweigart® Light Mocha Cashel Linen® (28 ct). It was stitched over 2 fabric threads. Three strands of floss were used for Cross Stitch and Backstitch, unless otherwise noted in the color key. Attach beads using 1 strand of DMC ecru floss for white beads and 1 strand of DMC 498 floss for red beads.

For ornament, trim stitched piece ³⁄₄" larger than design on all sides. Cut a piece of Light Mocha Cashel Linen® the same size as stitched piece for backing. Matching right sides and leaving an opening for turning, use a ¹⁄₂" seam allowance to sew fabric pieces together. Trim seam allowances diagonally at corners. Turn ornament right side out, carefully pushing corners outward. Stuff ornament with polyester fiberfill and blind stitch opening closed.

For hanger, refer to photo and tack one end of an 8" length of ¹⁄₄"w ribbon to top of ornament back at each corner. Tie ribbon in a bow; trim ends as desired.

Design by Joan E. Konyn.

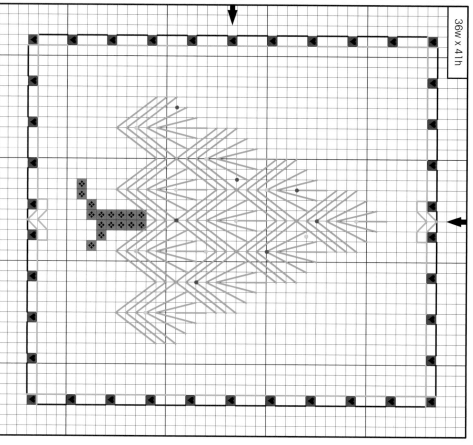

36w x 41h

X	DMC	B'ST	ANC.	COLOR
❖ ◩	ecru	◪*	ecru	ecru
	319	◩*	387	green
	498	*	218	green
●	801		1005	red
	Kreinik Fine Braid-002	◩*†	359	brown
● ◩	Mill Hill Bead - 03021			
◩	Mill Hill Bead - 62013			

* Work in long stitches.
† Use 1 strand of braid.

22

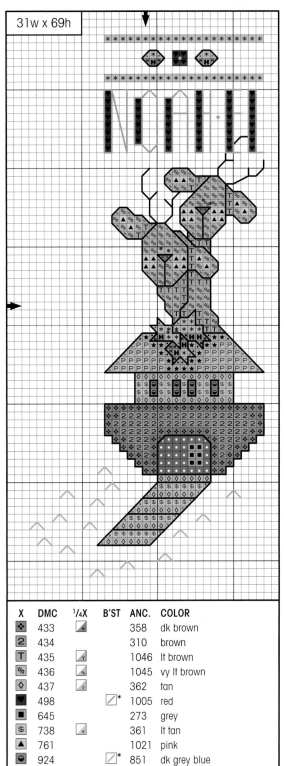

"Noah-el" Stocking

Invite holiday smiles with this cute pair of ark-riding reindeer! From their rooftop seat, they convey an amusing Noel message on a miniature stocking you can fill with candies or a tiny gift.

The design was stitched on a 6" x 9" piece of Antique White Cashel Linen® (28 ct). It was stitched over 2 fabric threads. Two strands of floss were used for Cross Stitch, 1 for Backstitch, and 3 for French Knots, unless otherwise noted in the color key. It was made into a stocking.

For stocking, you will need a 6" x 9" piece of Antique White Cashel Linen® for backing, tracing paper, pencil, fabric marking pencil, and a 5" length of ¹/₈" w ribbon for hanger.

For stocking pattern, trace pattern, pg. 145, onto tracing paper; add a ¹/₂" seam allowance on all sides and cut out. Referring to photo for placement, position pattern on wrong side of stitched piece; pin pattern in place. Use fabric marking pencil to draw around pattern; remove pattern and cut out on drawn line. Use pattern and cut one from backing fabric.

Matching right sides and leaving top edge open, use ¹/₂" seam allowance to sew stitched piece and backing fabric together. Turn top edge of stocking ¹/₂" to wrong side and hem. Clip seam allowance at curves and turn stocking right side out.

For hanger, fold ribbon in half. Referring to photo, tack to inside of stocking.

Design by Laurie Oksness.

X	DMC	¹/₄X	B'ST	ANC.	COLOR
❖	433	◢		358	dk brown
2	434			310	brown
T	435	◢T		1046	lt brown
%	436	◢		1045	vy lt brown
◇	437	◢		362	tan
▼	498		◢*	1005	red
■	645			273	grey
$	738	◢s		361	lt tan
▲	761			1021	pink
◐	924		◢*	851	dk grey blue
★	926	◢		850	grey blue
P	927	◢P		848	lt grey blue
H	986	◢H		246	green
✳	987	◢		244	lt green
▣	3371	◢	◢†	382	vy dk brown
●	498		red French Knot		
●*	739		vy lt tan French Knot		
●	986		green French Knot		
●▲	3371		vy dk brown French Knot		

* Use 2 strands of floss.

† Use 2 strands of floss for antlers.

▲ Use 1 strand of floss.

31w x 69h

23

A Merry Assortment

Spread a little Christmas magic by dressing your tree in this set of quick-to-stitch designs. The merry assortment of trims features your favorite Yuletide symbols, including a pair of bells to ring in the New Year.

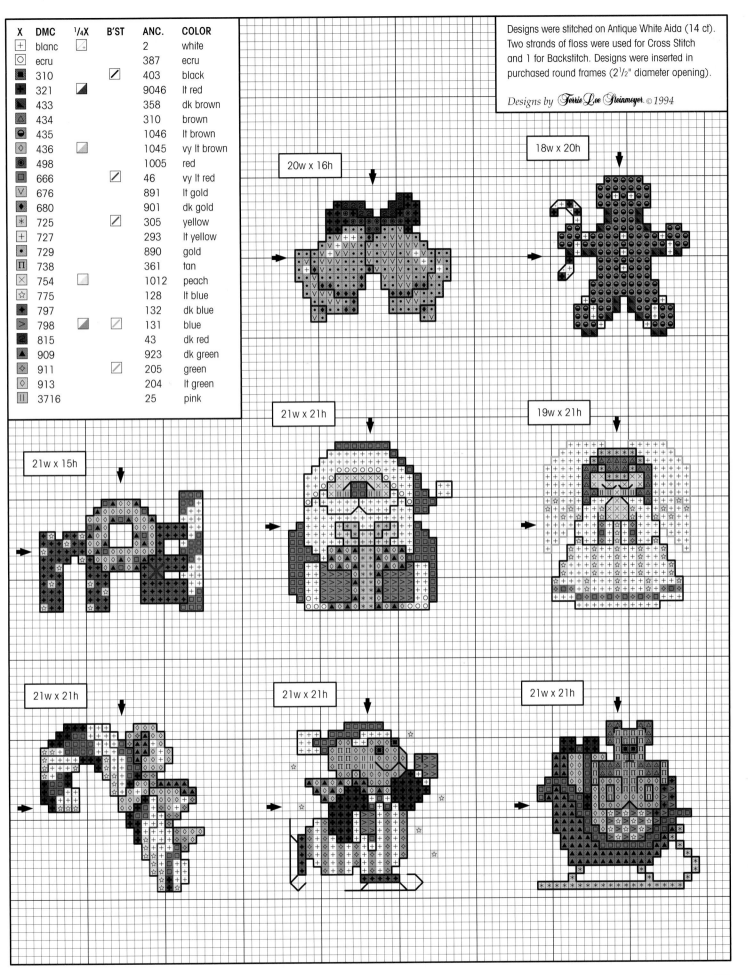

X	DMC	1/4X	B'ST	ANC.	COLOR
+	blanc			2	white
○	ecru			387	ecru
■	310		✓	403	black
◢	321	◢		9046	lt red
◤	433			358	dk brown
▲	434			310	brown
◖	435			1046	lt brown
◇	436	◩		1045	vy lt brown
◉	498			1005	red
▣	666		✓	46	vy lt red
V	676			891	lt gold
◆	680			901	dk gold
✳	725		✓	305	yellow
⊞	727			293	lt yellow
•	729			890	gold
∏	738			361	tan
✕	754	◨		1012	peach
☆	775			128	lt blue
◆	797			132	dk blue
➤	798	◢	✓	131	blue
▨	815			43	dk red
▲	909			923	dk green
◇	911		✓	205	green
◇	913			204	lt green
‖	3716			25	pink

Designs were stitched on Antique White Aida (14 ct).
Two strands of floss were used for Cross Stitch
and 1 for Backstitch. Designs were inserted in
purchased round frames (2 1/2" diameter opening).

Designs by Terrie Lee Steinmeyer. © 1994

20w x 16h

18w x 20h

21w x 15h

21w x 21h

19w x 21h

21w x 21h

21w x 21h

21w x 21h

25

Divine Ornaments

Share glad tidings and divine details of the Savior's birth with all who behold the boughs of your tree. Our exquisitely embellished ornaments combine popular passages of scripture, bright beading, and lavish cording for heirlooms your family will hold seasonally sacred for Christmases to come.

THE GLORY OF THE LORD SHONE ROUND ABOUT THEM
LUKE 2:9

On Earth Peace, Good Will Toward Men
LUKE 2:14

unto us a child is born
Isaiah 9:6

GOOD TIDINGS of GREAT JOY
LUKE 2:10

GLORY TO GOD IN THE HIGHEST
LUKE 2:14

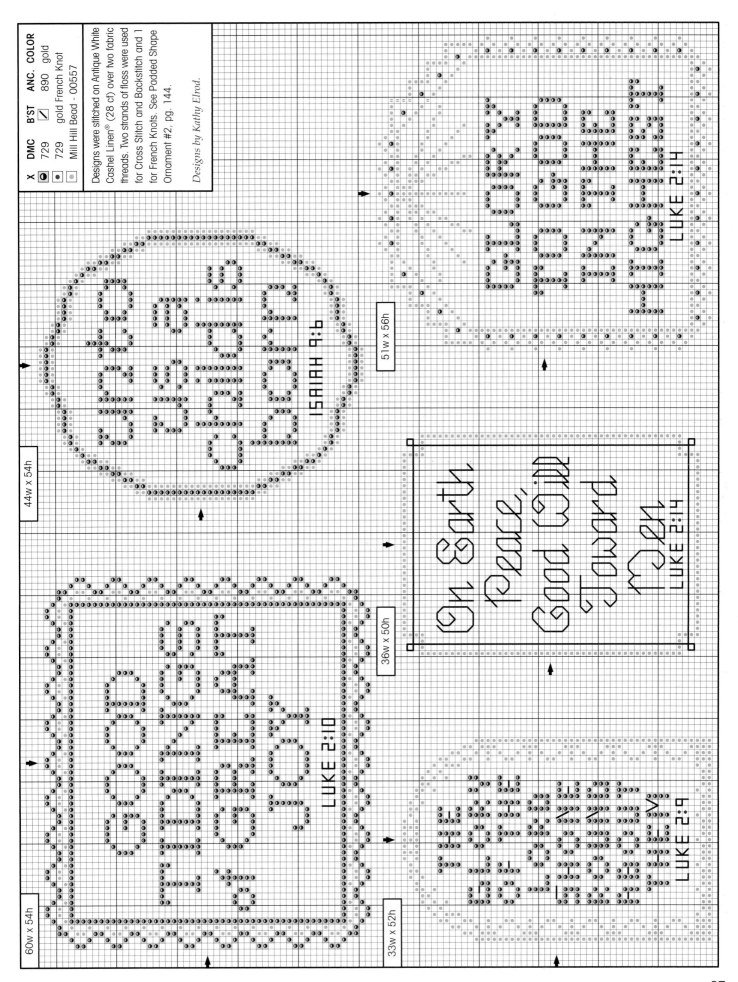

Tidings of Good Cheer

*Whimsical characters team with merry messages to create these cheery tree trimmers finished with
a festive fabric edging. Their circular shape also makes them good choices for topping jars.*

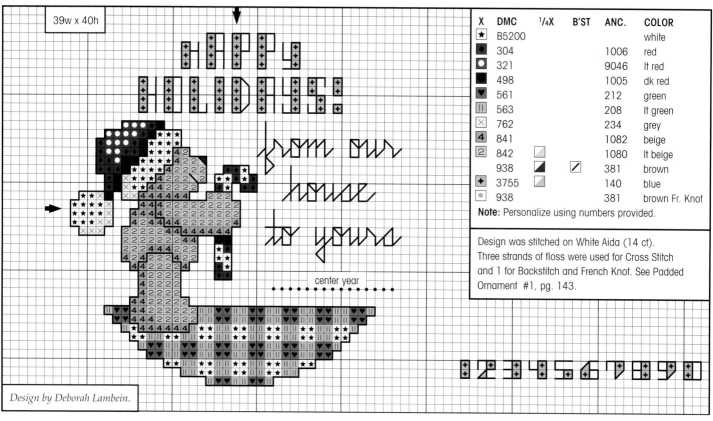

39w x 40h

X	DMC	1/4X	B'ST	ANC.	COLOR
★	B5200				white
◆	304			1006	red
◖	321			9046	lt red
■	498			1005	dk red
♥	561			212	green
‖	563			208	lt green
✕	762			234	grey
4	841			1082	beige
2	842	◪		1080	lt beige
	938	◣	╱	381	brown
✦	3755	◪		140	blue
●	938			381	brown Fr. Knot

Note: Personalize using numbers provided.

Design was stitched on White Aida (14 ct).
Three strands of floss were used for Cross Stitch
and 1 for Backstitch and French Knot. See Padded
Ornament #1, pg. 143.

center year

Design by Deborah Lambein.

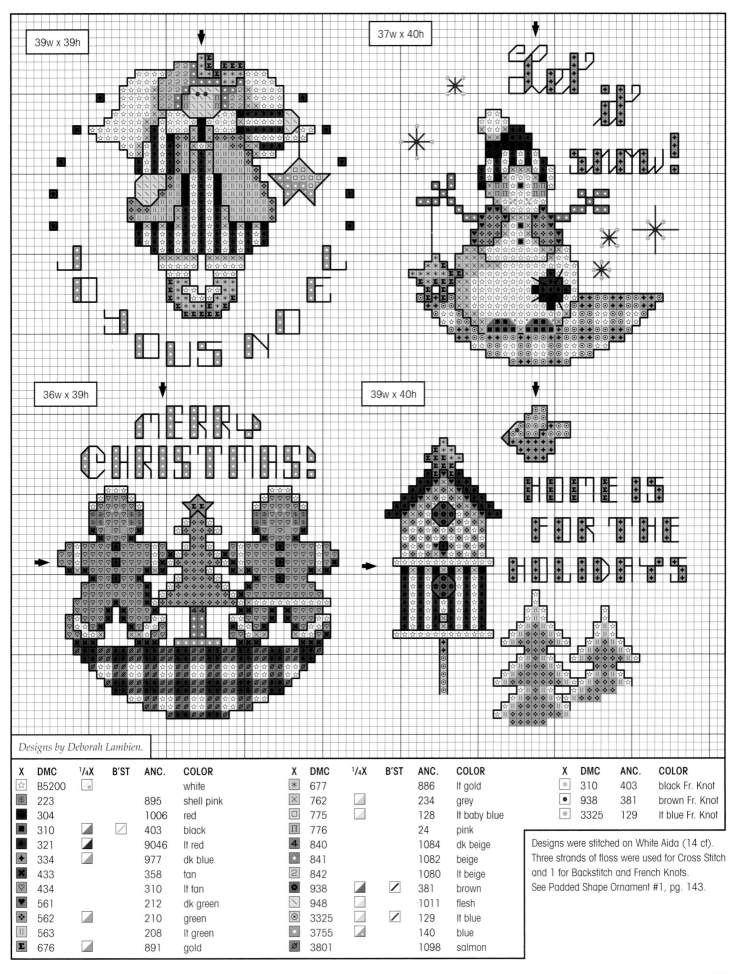

39w x 39h
37w x 40h
36w x 39h
39w x 40h
MERRY CHRISTMAS!
HOME IS FOR THE HOLIDAYS

Designs by Deborah Lambien.

X	DMC	1/4X	B'ST	ANC.	COLOR
☆	B5200	☆			white
	223			895	shell pink
	304			1006	red
■	310	◢	/	403	black
	321	◢		9046	lt red
✦	334	◢		977	dk blue
✖	433			358	tan
♡	434			310	lt tan
♥	561			212	dk green
❖	562	◢		210	green
‖	563			208	lt green
Σ	676	◢		891	gold

X	DMC	1/4X	B'ST	ANC.	COLOR
✳	677			886	lt gold
×	762	◢		234	grey
□	775	◢		128	lt baby blue
Π	776			24	pink
4	840			1084	dk beige
•	841			1082	beige
2	842			1080	lt beige
⬟	938	◢	/	381	brown
\	948	◢		1011	flesh
◎	3325	◢	/	129	lt blue
•	3755	◢		140	blue
∅	3801			1098	salmon

X	DMC	ANC.	COLOR
•	310	403	black Fr. Knot
•	938	381	brown Fr. Knot
•	3325	129	lt blue Fr. Knot

Designs were stitched on White Aida (14 ct). Three strands of floss were used for Cross Stitch and 1 for Backstitch and French Knots. See Padded Shape Ornament #1, pg. 143.

Merry Mice

You won't mind having a mouse in the house when you decorate the tree with these merrymaking mice! The adorable critters are captured in a series of holiday scenes fashioned into easy-to-make decorations.

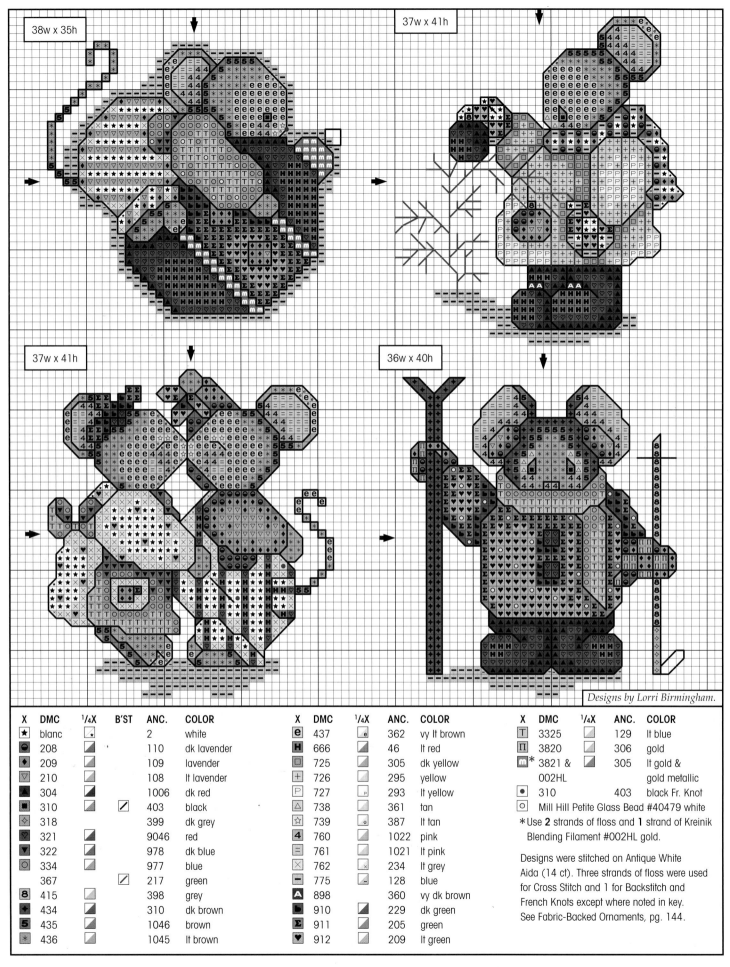

Designs by Lorri Birmingham.

X	DMC	¼X	B'ST	ANC.	COLOR
★	blanc			2	white
◒	208			110	dk lavender
◆	209			109	lavender
▽	210			108	lt lavender
◣	304			1006	dk red
■	310		╱	403	black
◈	318			399	dk grey
▼	321			9046	red
▼	322			978	dk blue
◎	334			977	blue
	367		╱	217	green
8	415			398	grey
◆	434			310	dk brown
5	435			1046	brown
*	436			1045	lt brown

X	DMC	¼X	ANC.	COLOR
e	437	e	362	vy lt brown
H	666		46	lt red
▢	725		305	dk yellow
+	726		295	yellow
P	727	P	293	lt yellow
△	738		361	tan
☆	739	☆	387	lt tan
4	760		1022	pink
=	761		1021	lt pink
✕	762	×	234	lt grey
−	775	-	128	blue
A	898		360	vy dk brown
◣	910		229	dk green
Σ	911		205	green
♥	912		209	lt green

X	DMC	¼X	ANC.	COLOR
T	3325		129	lt blue
Π	3820		306	gold
m*	3821 & 002HL		305	lt gold & gold metallic
●	310		403	black Fr. Knot
○	Mill Hill Petite Glass Bead #40479 white			

*Use **2** strands of floss and **1** strand of Kreinik Blending Filament #002HL gold.

Designs were stitched on Antique White Aida (14 ct). Three strands of floss were used for Cross Stitch and 1 for Backstitch and French Knots except where noted in key. See Fabric-Backed Ornaments, pg. 144.

X	DMC	1/4X	B'ST	ANC.	COLOR
★	blanc			2	white
◆	209			109	lavender
▽	210			108	lt lavender
◼	304			1006	dk red
◼	310		/	403	black
◇	318			399	grey
▨	321			9046	red
▼	322			978	dk blue
○	334			977	blue
B	414			235	dk grey
5	435			1046	dk brown
✳	436			1045	brown
e	437			362	lt brown
H	666			46	lt red
▢	725			305	dk yellow
+	726			295	yellow
P	727			293	lt yellow
☆	739			387	tan
4	760			1022	pink
=	761			1021	lt pink
✕	762			234	lt grey
−	775			128	vy lt blue
◼	910			229	dk green
Σ	911			205	green
♥	912			209	lt green
T	3325			129	lt blue
m *	3821 & 002HL			305	gold & gold metallic
●	310			403	black Fr. Knot
○	Mill Hill Petite Glass Bead #40479 white				

*Use **2** strands of floss and **1** strand of Kreinik Blending Filament #002HL gold.

Designs were stitched on Antique White Aida (14 ct). Three strands of floss were used for Cross Stitch and 1 for Backstitch and French Knots except where noted in key. See Fabric-Backed Ornaments, pg. 144.

45w x 50h

35w x 52h

38w x 44h

Designs by Lorri Birmingham.

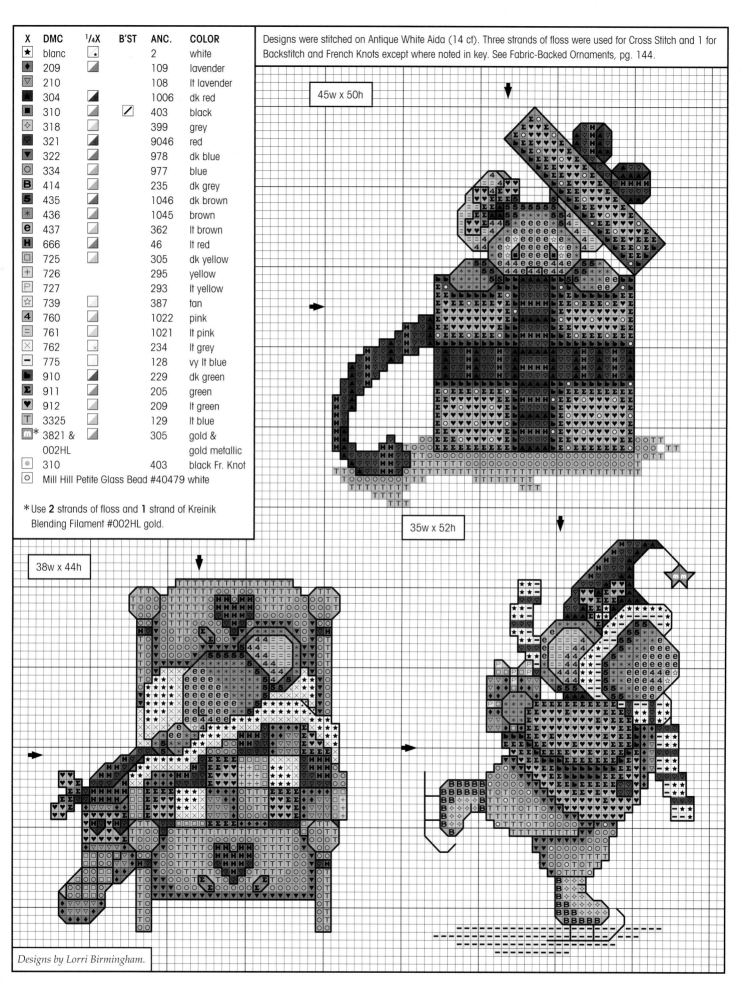

X	DMC	¼X	B'ST	ANC.	COLOR
★	blanc	·		2	white
◐	208	◣		110	dk lavender
◆	209	◣		109	lavender
▽	210	◣		108	lt lavender
▲	304	◣		1006	dk red
	310		╱	403	black
⊓	317	◣		400	grey
♥	321	◣	╱	9046	red
▼	322	◣		978	dk blue
◎	334	◣		977	blue
✿	413	◣		236	dk grey
B	414	◣		235	lt grey
5	435	◣		1046	dk brown
*	436	◣		1045	brown
e	437	e		362	lt brown
H	666	◣		46	lt red
✔	721			925	orange
□	725			305	yellow
P	727			293	lt yellow
△	738	☐		361	tan
☆	739			387	lt tan
4	760	◣		1022	pink
▤	761	◣		1021	lt pink
−	775	-		128	vy lt blue
◧	910	◣		229	dk green
Σ	911	◣		205	green
♥	912	◣		209	lt green
T	3325	◣		129	lt blue
m*	3821 &	◣		305	gold &
	002HL				gold metallic
●	310			403	black Fr. Knot
◎	Mill Hill Petite Glass Bead #40479 white				

*Use **2** strands of floss and **1** strand of
Kreinik Blending Filament #002HL gold.

Designs were stitched on Antique White Aida (14 ct).
Three strands of floss were used for Cross Stitch and 1
for Backstitch and French Knots except where noted in
key. See Fabric-Backed Ornaments, pg. 144.

50w x 49h

44w x 53h

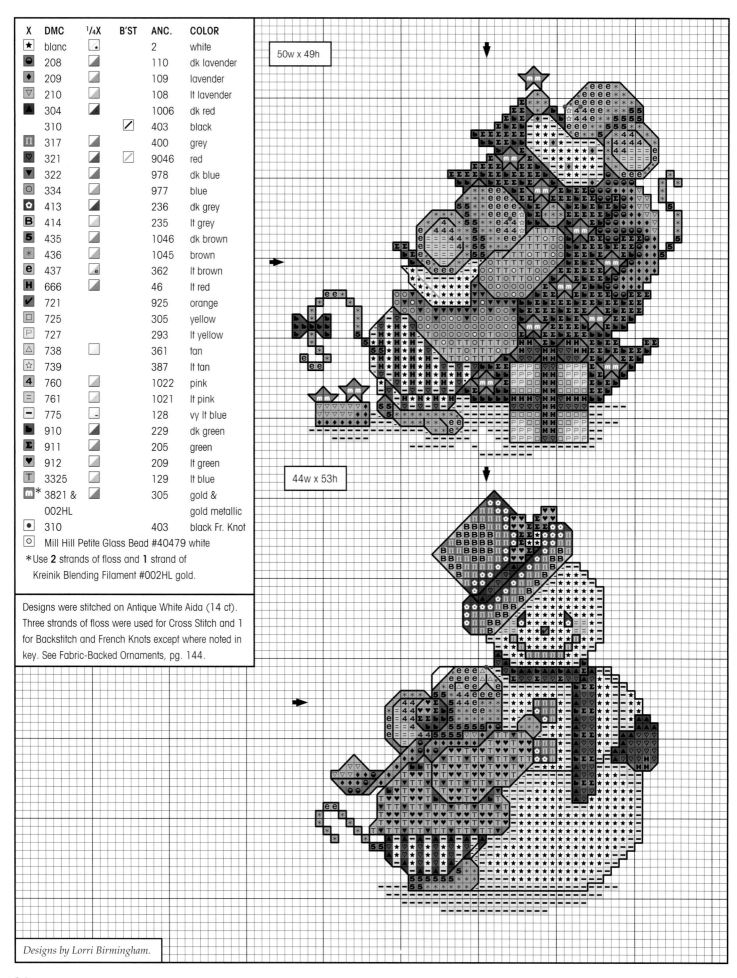

Designs by Lorri Birmingham.

Teeny-Tiny Tree Trims

A tabletop tree will look even merrier decked with our holiday collection of teeny-tiny trims. Featuring darling little images and cute phrases, these ornaments can also add bits of Christmas cheer to gifts, wreaths, garlands, and more.

Each design was stitched on a 4" x 6" piece of Zweigart® Ivory Aida (14 ct). Two strands of floss were used for Cross Stitch and 1 for Backstitch and French Knots, unless otherwise noted in the color key. They were made into ornaments.

For each ornament, you will need a 1³⁄₄" length of ¹⁄₈" dia. wooden dowel and a 7" length of floss for hanger.

Trim stitched piece to measure 1³⁄₄" x 4³⁄₄" allowing a ¹⁄₂" margin at bottom of design, ³⁄₈" margins at sides of design, and a 2³⁄₄" margin at top of design.

Turn each long edge of ornament ¹⁄₄" to wrong side and press. Matching wrong sides and short edges, fold ornament in half. To form a casing, machine stitch ornament ¹⁄₄" from fold. Machine stitch ³⁄₈" from bottom edges; fringe to within 2 fabric threads of stitching. Insert dowel in casing; add floss hanger.

X	DMC	¹⁄₄X	B'ST	ANC.	COLOR
•	blanc	•	*†	2	white
	310		/	403	black
▼	321	◢	/	9046	red
T	436	◿		1045	tan
⊖	725	⊙		305	dk yellow
$	726	s		295	yellow
	740		/	316	orange
✳	762	*		234	vy lt grey
	783		/†	306	gold
%	813			161	lt blue
▣	824	◿		164	dk blue
✥	826			161	blue
H	910	◪	/	229	green
P	948	p		1011	flesh
•	blanc		white French Knot		
⊙	310		black French Knot		
⊙	321		red French Knot		

* For "Homemade," use 2 strands of floss.

† Work in long stitches.

Designs by Kathy Elrod.

Wee Stockings

A tabletop tree is the perfect showcase for these wee stocking ornaments stitched on perforated plastic. Why not slip one in with your greeting cards, as well, for a sweet surprise.

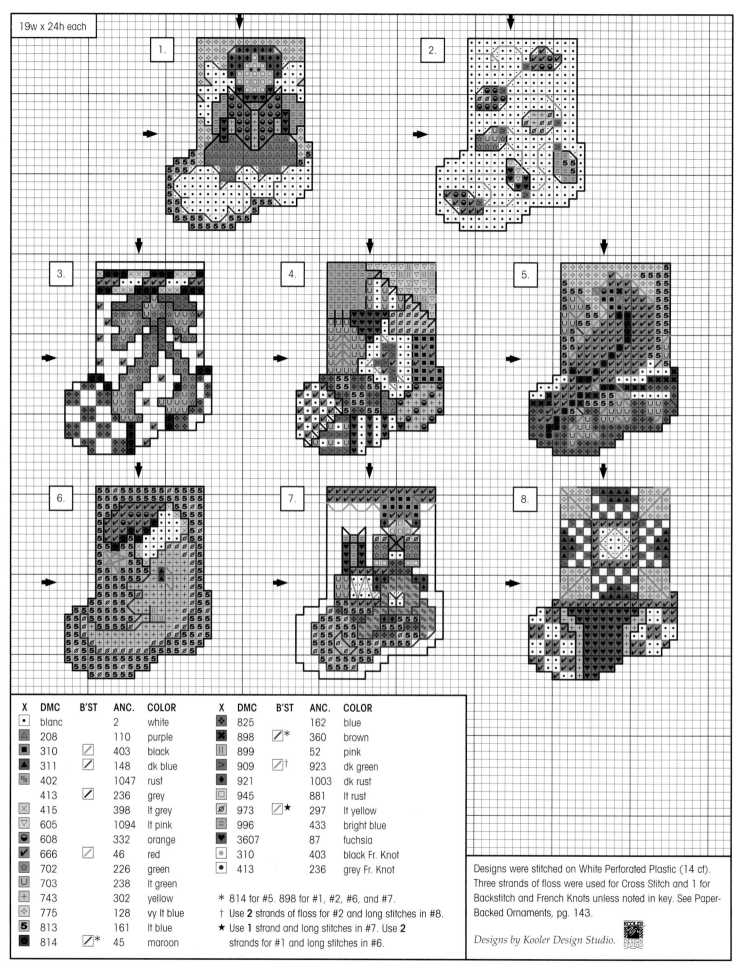

19w x 24h each

X	DMC	B'ST	ANC.	COLOR		X	DMC	B'ST	ANC.	COLOR
•	blanc		2	white		❖	825		162	blue
△	208		110	purple		✖	898	╱*	360	brown
■	310	╱	403	black		‖	899		52	pink
▲	311	╱	148	dk blue		▷	909	╱†	923	dk green
‰	402		1047	rust		◆	921		1003	dk rust
	413	╱	236	grey		▢	945		881	lt rust
✕	415		398	lt grey		∅	973	╱★	297	lt yellow
▽	605		1094	lt pink		═	996		433	bright blue
◒	608		332	orange		♥	3607		87	fuchsia
✔	666	╱	46	red		●	310		403	black Fr. Knot
☆	702		226	green		●	413		236	grey Fr. Knot
U	703		238	lt green						
+	743		302	yellow						
◇	775		128	vy lt blue						
5	813		161	lt blue						
■	814	╱*	45	maroon						

* 814 for #5. 898 for #1, #2, #6, and #7.

† Use **2** strands of floss for #2 and long stitches in #8.

★ Use **1** strand and long stitches in #7. Use **2**
strands for #1 and long stitches in #6.

Designs were stitched on White Perforated Plastic (14 ct).
Three strands of floss were used for Cross Stitch and 1 for
Backstitch and French Knots unless noted in key. See Paper-
Backed Ornaments, pg. 143.

Designs by Kooler Design Studio.

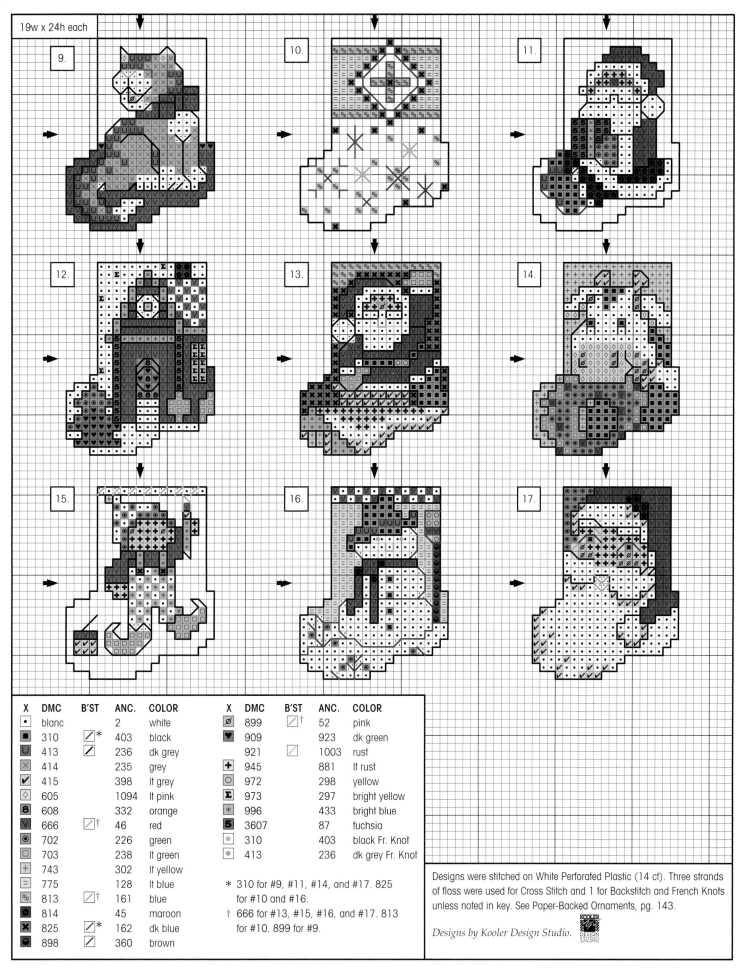

19w x 24h each

X	DMC	B'ST	ANC.	COLOR
•	blanc		2	white
■	310	⟋*	403	black
U	413	⟋	236	dk grey
✕	414		235	grey
✔	415		398	lt grey
◇	605		1094	lt pink
8	608		332	orange
▼	666	⟋†	46	red
◉	702		226	green
▢	703		238	lt green
✚	743		302	lt yellow
＝	775		128	lt blue
%	813	⟋†	161	blue
●	814		45	maroon
✕	825	⟋*	162	dk blue
●	898	⟋	360	brown

X	DMC	B'ST	ANC.	COLOR
∅	899	⟋†	52	pink
♥	909		923	dk green
	921		1003	rust
+	945	⟋	881	lt rust
○	972		298	yellow
Σ	973		297	bright yellow
*	996		433	bright blue
5	3607		87	fuchsia
●	310		403	black Fr. Knot
●	413		236	dk grey Fr. Knot

* 310 for #9, #11, #14, and #17. 825
for #10 and #16.

† 666 for #13, #15, #16, and #17. 813
for #10. 899 for #9.

Designs were stitched on White Perforated Plastic (14 ct). Three strands of floss were used for Cross Stitch and 1 for Backstitch and French Knots unless noted in key. See Paper-Backed Ornaments, pg. 143.

Designs by Kooler Design Studio.

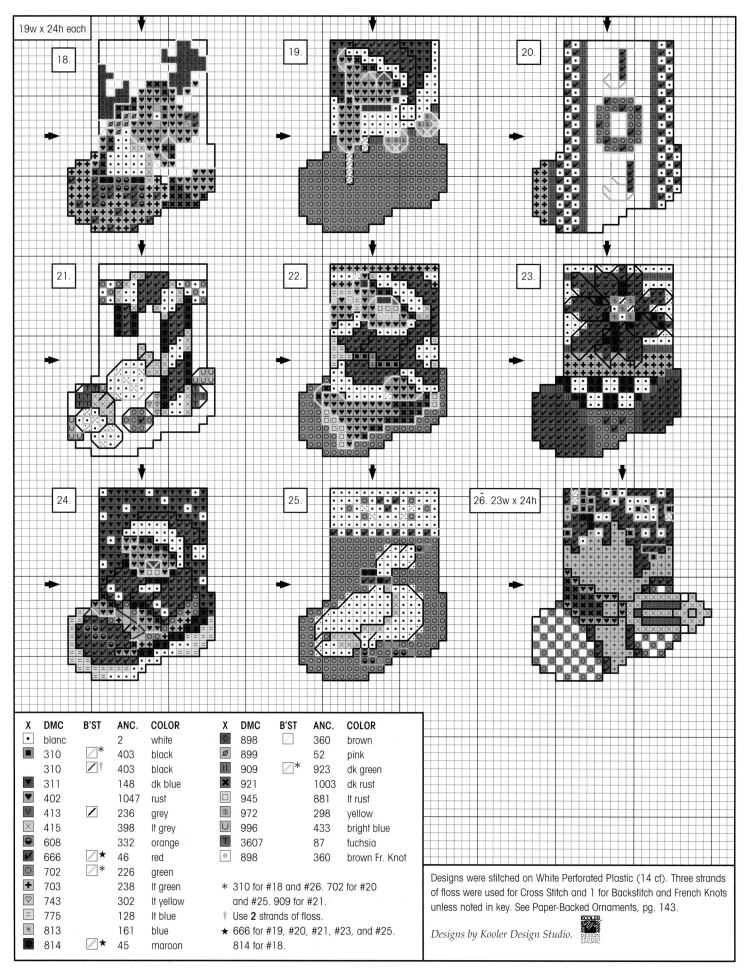

X	DMC	B'ST	ANC.	COLOR	X	DMC	B'ST	ANC.	COLOR
•	blanc		2	white	◆	898	◪	360	brown
■	310	◪*	403	black	ø	899		52	pink
	310	◪†	403	black	‖	909	◪*	923	dk green
▼	311		148	dk blue	✕	921		1003	dk rust
♥	402		1047	rust	▢	945		881	lt rust
V	413	◪	236	grey	$	972		298	yellow
✕	415		398	lt grey	U	996		433	bright blue
◓	608		332	orange	T	3607		87	fuchsia
◪	666	◪★	46	red	◉	898		360	brown Fr. Knot
◉	702	◪*	226	green					
+	703		238	lt green					
♡	743		302	lt yellow	* 310 for #18 and #26. 702 for #20				
▤	775		128	lt blue	and #25. 909 for #21.				
✳	813		161	blue	† Use **2** strands of floss.				
◼	814	◪★	45	maroon	★ 666 for #19, #20, #21, #23, and #25.				
					814 for #18.				

Designs were stitched on White Perforated Plastic (14 ct). Three strands of floss were used for Cross Stitch and 1 for Backstitch and French Knots unless noted in key. See Paper-Backed Ornaments, pg. 143.

Designs by Kooler Design Studio.

Festive Medley

Imagine the fun you'll have thinking of ways to display this festive medley of motifs. The tiny treasures can be used in a variety of fun finishes from ornaments and package ties to bread cloths and towel embellishments.

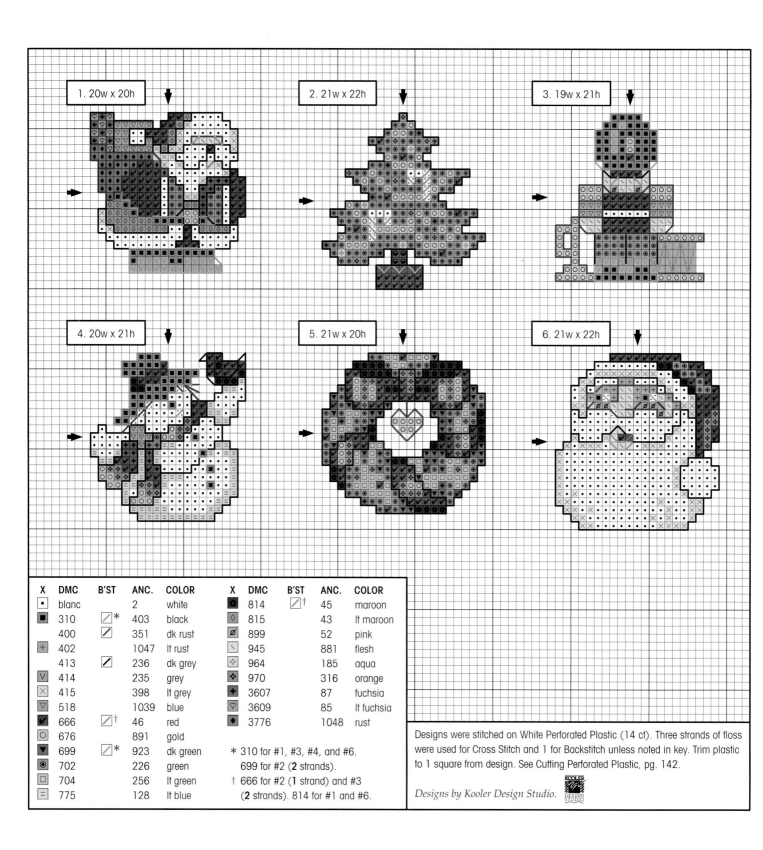

X	DMC	B'ST	ANC.	COLOR	X	DMC	B'ST	ANC.	COLOR
•	blanc		2	white	●	814	◪†	45	maroon
■	310	◪*	403	black	◇	815		43	lt maroon
	400	◪	351	dk rust	∅	899		52	pink
+	402		1047	lt rust	＼	945		881	flesh
	413	◪	236	dk grey	◈	964		185	aqua
∇	414		235	grey	❖	970		316	orange
✕	415		398	lt grey	✦	3607		87	fuchsia
▽	518		1039	blue	♡	3609		85	lt fuchsia
◪	666	◪†	46	red	◆	3776		1048	rust
○	676		891	gold					
▼	699	◪*	923	dk green	* 310 for #1, #3, #4, and #6.
◉	702		226	green	699 for #2 (**2** strands).
▢	704		256	lt green	† 666 for #2 (**1** strand) and #3
=	775		128	lt blue	(**2** strands). 814 for #1 and #6.

Designs were stitched on White Perforated Plastic (14 ct). Three strands of floss were used for Cross Stitch and 1 for Backstitch unless noted in key. Trim plastic to 1 square from design. See Cutting Perforated Plastic, pg. 142.

Designs by Kooler Design Studio.

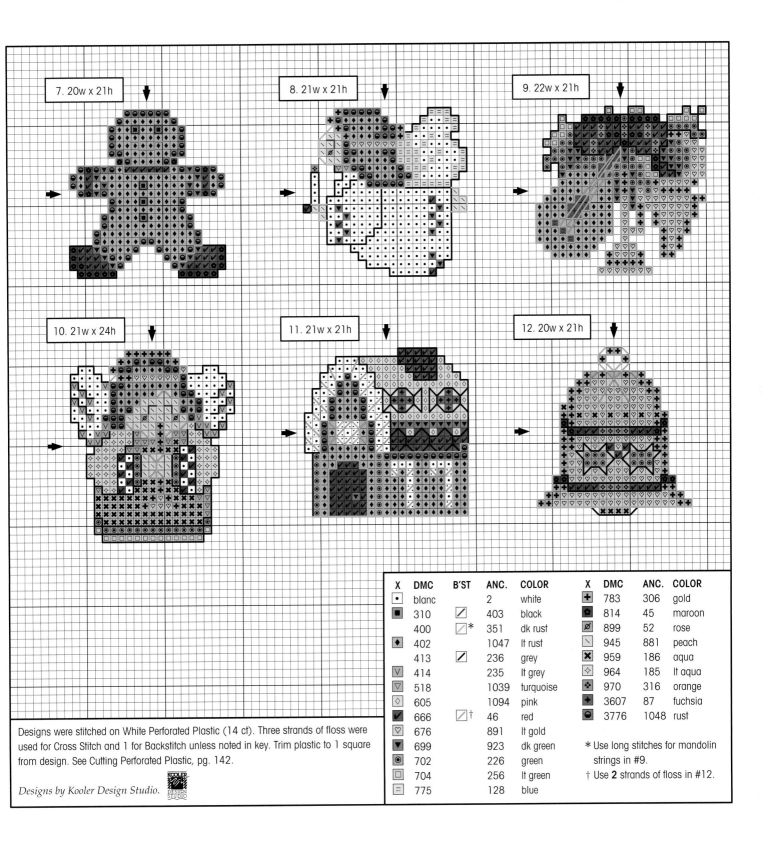

7. 20w x 21h

8. 21w x 21h

9. 22w x 21h

10. 21w x 24h

11. 21w x 21h

12. 20w x 21h

X	DMC	B'ST	ANC.	COLOR	X	DMC	ANC.	COLOR
•	blanc		2	white	✚	783	306	gold
■	310	╱	403	black	⬢	814	45	maroon
	400	╱*	351	dk rust	⊘	899	52	rose
◆	402		1047	lt rust	⃥	945	881	peach
	413	╱	236	grey	✖	959	186	aqua
∨	414		235	lt grey	◇	964	185	lt aqua
▽	518		1039	turquoise	✾	970	316	orange
◇	605		1094	pink	✦	3607	87	fuchsia
♡	666	╱†	46	red	◓	3776	1048	rust
◪	676		891	lt gold				
▼	699		923	dk green	* Use long stitches for mandolin			
◉	702		226	green	strings in #9.			
▢	704		256	lt green	† Use **2** strands of floss in #12.			
═	775		128	blue				

Designs were stitched on White Perforated Plastic (14 ct). Three strands of floss were used for Cross Stitch and 1 for Backstitch unless noted in key. Trim plastic to 1 square from design. See Cutting Perforated Plastic, pg. 142.

Designs by Kooler Design Studio.

flying Favorites

Add this whimsical trio to the tree and they'll soar to the top of your favorite ornament list! Suspended from ribbon hangers, Santa and his pals take to the air.

56w x 53h

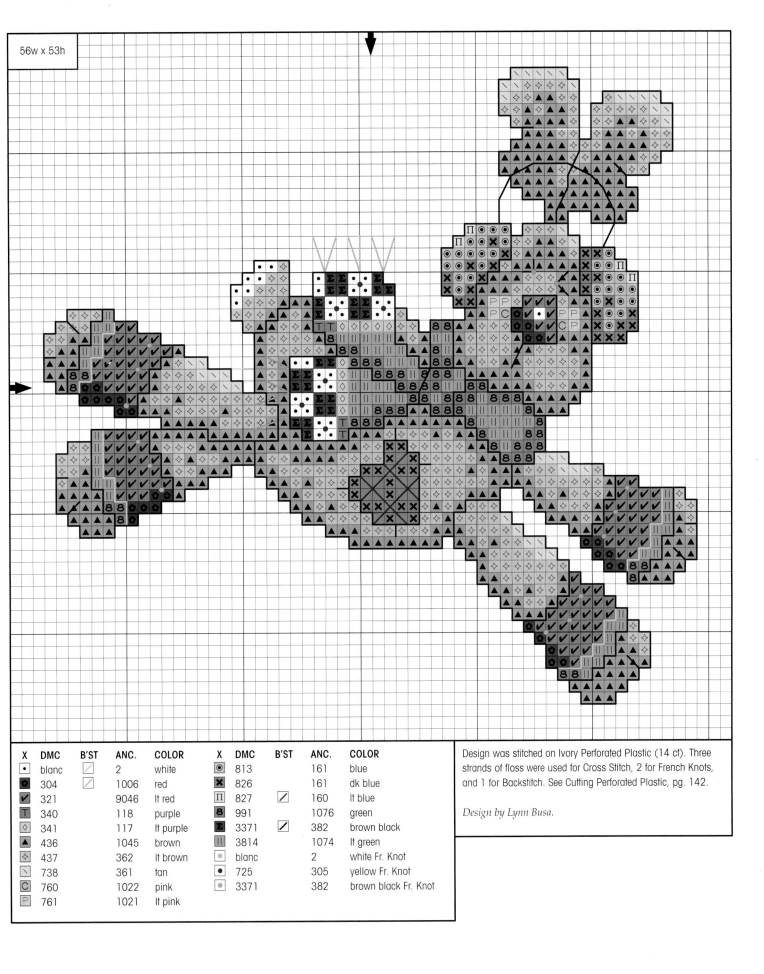

X	DMC	B'ST	ANC.	COLOR		X	DMC	B'ST	ANC.	COLOR
•	blanc	/	2	white		◉	813		161	blue
✿	304	/	1006	red		✕	826		161	dk blue
✔	321		9046	lt red		Π	827	/	160	lt blue
T	340		118	purple		8	991		1076	green
◇	341		117	lt purple		Σ	3371	/	382	brown black
▲	436		1045	brown		‖	3814		1074	lt green
✧	437		362	lt brown		◦	blanc		2	white Fr. Knot
\	738		361	tan		•	725		305	yellow Fr. Knot
C	760		1022	pink		◦	3371		382	brown black Fr. Knot
P	761		1021	lt pink						

Design was stitched on Ivory Perforated Plastic (14 ct). Three strands of floss were used for Cross Stitch, 2 for French Knots, and 1 for Backstitch. See Cutting Perforated Plastic, pg. 142.

Design by Lynn Busa.

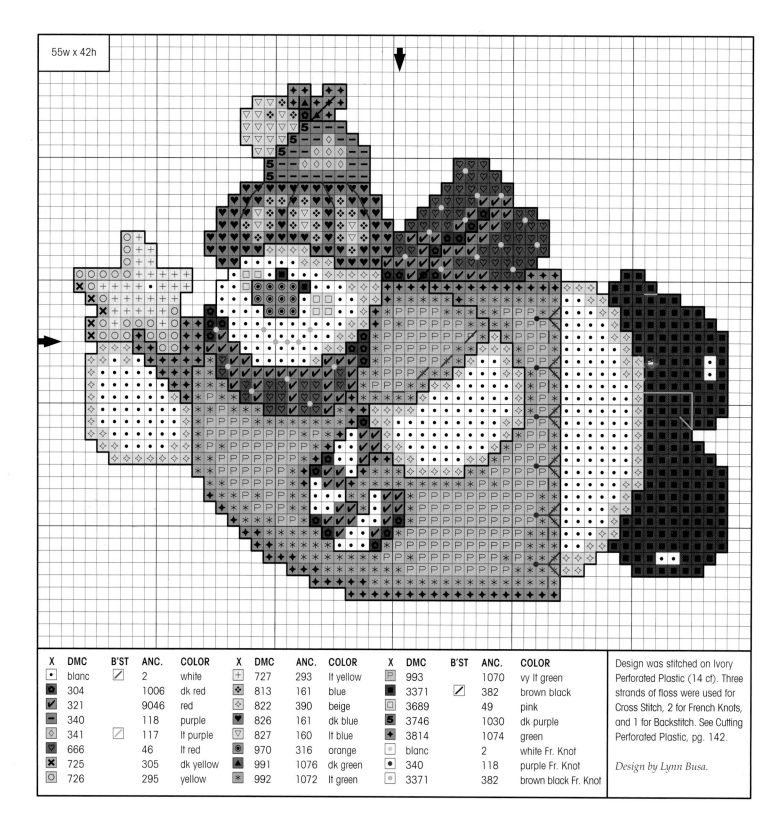

55w x 42h

X	DMC	B'ST	ANC.	COLOR	X	DMC	ANC.	COLOR	X	DMC	B'ST	ANC.	COLOR
•	blanc	✓	2	white	+	727	293	lt yellow	P	993		1070	vy lt green
⬟	304		1006	dk red	❖	813	161	blue	■	3371	✓	382	brown black
✔	321		9046	red	◇	822	390	beige	▫	3689		49	pink
−	340		118	purple	♥	826	161	dk blue	5	3746		1030	dk purple
◇	341	✓	117	lt purple	▽	827	160	lt blue	✦	3814		1074	green
▼	666		46	lt red	◉	970	316	orange	○	blanc		2	white Fr. Knot
✖	725		305	dk yellow	▲	991	1076	dk green	•	340		118	purple Fr. Knot
○	726		295	yellow	✳	992	1072	lt green	●	3371		382	brown black Fr. Knot

Design was stitched on Ivory Perforated Plastic (14 ct). Three strands of floss were used for Cross Stitch, 2 for French Knots, and 1 for Backstitch. See Cutting Perforated Plastic, pg. 142.

Design by Lynn Busa.

56w x 44h

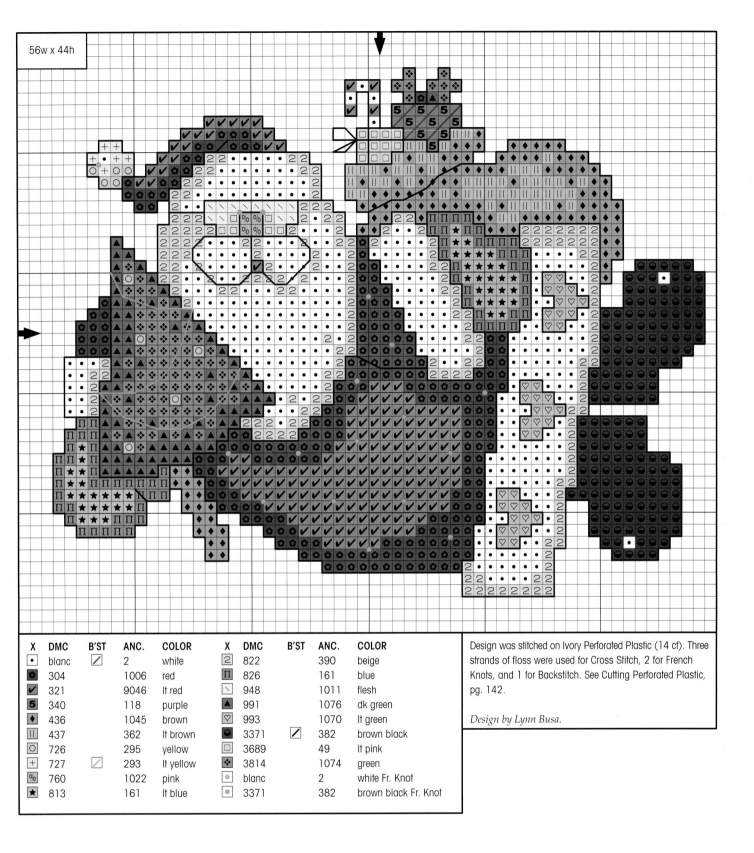

X	DMC	B'ST	ANC.	COLOR	X	DMC	B'ST	ANC.	COLOR
•	blanc	⁄	2	white	2	822		390	beige
✿	304		1006	red	∏	826		161	blue
✔	321		9046	lt red	＼	948		1011	flesh
5	340		118	purple	▲	991		1076	dk green
◆	436		1045	brown	♡	993		1070	lt green
‖	437		362	lt brown	◼	3371	⁄	382	brown black
○	726		295	yellow	▢	3689		49	lt pink
+	727	⁄	293	lt yellow	✤	3814		1074	green
%	760		1022	pink	●	blanc		2	white Fr. Knot
★	813		161	lt blue	●	3371		382	brown black Fr. Knot

Design was stitched on Ivory Perforated Plastic (14 ct). Three strands of floss were used for Cross Stitch, 2 for French Knots, and 1 for Backstitch. See Cutting Perforated Plastic, pg. 142.

Design by Lynn Busa.

Santa Collection

These Santa ornaments are a must for collectors! They depict three old-fashioned portraits of the jolly old gent wrapped in rich red robes and laden with toy-filled knapsacks.

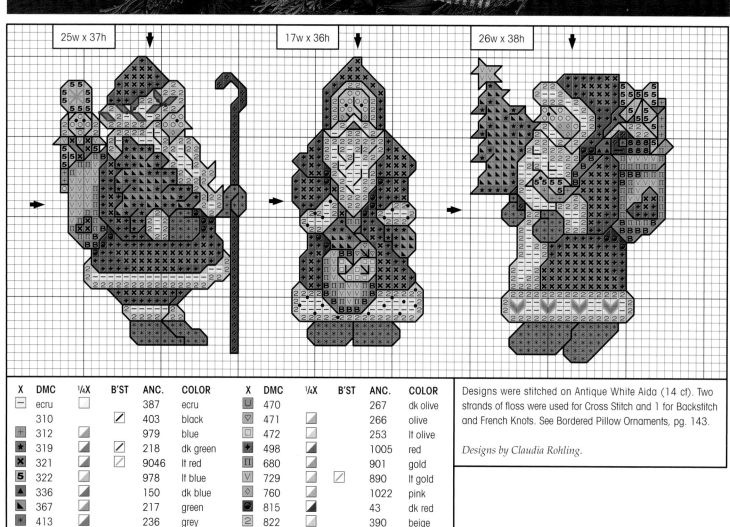

X	DMC	¼X	B'ST	ANC.	COLOR	X	DMC	¼X	B'ST	ANC.	COLOR
−	ecru			387	ecru	U	470			267	dk olive
	310		╱	403	black	♥	471	╱		266	olive
+	312	╱		979	blue		472	╱		253	lt olive
★	319	╱	╱	218	dk green	✦	498	╱		1005	red
✕	321	╱	╱	9046	lt red	Π	680	╱		901	gold
5	322	╱		978	lt blue	V	729	╱	╱	890	lt gold
▲	336	╱		150	dk blue	◇	760	╱		1022	pink
◣	367	╱		217	green	◑	815	╱		43	dk red
✳	413	╱		236	grey	2	822	╱		390	beige
B	420	╱		374	dk gold	O	3779	╱		1012	peach
✿	433	╱		358	brown	●	310 black French Knot				
8	434			310	lt brown	●	321 lt red French Knot				

Designs were stitched on Antique White Aida (14 ct). Two strands of floss were used for Cross Stitch and 1 for Backstitch and French Knots. See Bordered Pillow Ornaments, pg. 143.

Designs by Claudia Rohling.

Christmas Sampler

Embellished with traditional Yuletide motifs arranged in sampler style, this miniature stocking will make a lovely keepsake or gift.

46w x 95h

X	DMC	B'ST	COLOR
☆	blanc		white
◆	304		red
■	310		black
⬭	501		green
$	729		gold
8	815		dk red
◉	840		brown
	930	/	blue
	938	/	dk brown
△	951		flesh

Design was stitched on an 8" x 12" piece of Antique White Aida (18 ct). Two strands of floss were used for Cross Stitch and 1 for Backstitch. It was made into a stocking ornament.

To finish stocking, cut a piece of evenweave fabric same size as stitched piece for backing. Matching right sides and leaving top edge open, sew front and back together just outside backstitch around outer edge of design. Trim top edge of stocking 1" away from design. Trim away remaining excess fabric leaving a ¼" seam allowance. Clip seam allowances at curves. Turn stocking right side out. Turn top edge to wrong side and tack in place. Add hanger if desired.

Design by Penny Duff.

Childhood Wonders

A joy to stitch, these precious pillow ornaments remind us of our childlike wonder for the holiday and the never-ending delights of the season.

X	DMC	¼X	ANC.	COLOR		X	DMC	¼X	ANC.	COLOR		X	DMC	¼X	ANC.	COLOR		X	DMC	¼X	B'ST	ANC.	COLOR
☆	blanc	☆	2	white		▲	645		273	grey		✔	931			1034	lt grey blue
◇	211		342	lt lavender		C	647		1040	lt grey		+	948			1011	lt peach
✚	304		1006	red		Π	676		891	gold		⊘	3325			129	blue
■	310		403	black		◣	676 &		891	gold &			3371		╱	382	brown black
◎	320		215	green			002			gold metallic		◥	3712			1023	pink
✳	321		9046	lt red		□	677		886	lt gold		●	209			109	lavender Fr. Knot
H	353		6	dk peach		T	721		925	orange		●	3371			382	brown black Fr. Knot
◐	367		217	dk green		P	722		323	lt orange
△	368		214	lt green		Σ	726		295	yellow
■	433		358	dk brown		◆	729		890	dk gold
♥	435		1046	brown		✖	754		1012	peach
3	437		362	lt brown		U	781		308	topaz
⬠	501		878	dk blue green		%	783		306	lt topaz
4	502		877	blue green		✔	928		274	blue grey
2	503		876	lt blue green		◉	930		1035	grey blue

* Use **2** strands of floss and **1** strand of gold metallic.

Designs were stitched on Ivory Aida (14 ct). Three strands of floss were used for Cross Stitch and 1 for Backstitch and French Knots except where noted in key. See Fringed Pillow Ornament, pg. 143 and Corded Pillow Ornament, pg. 143.

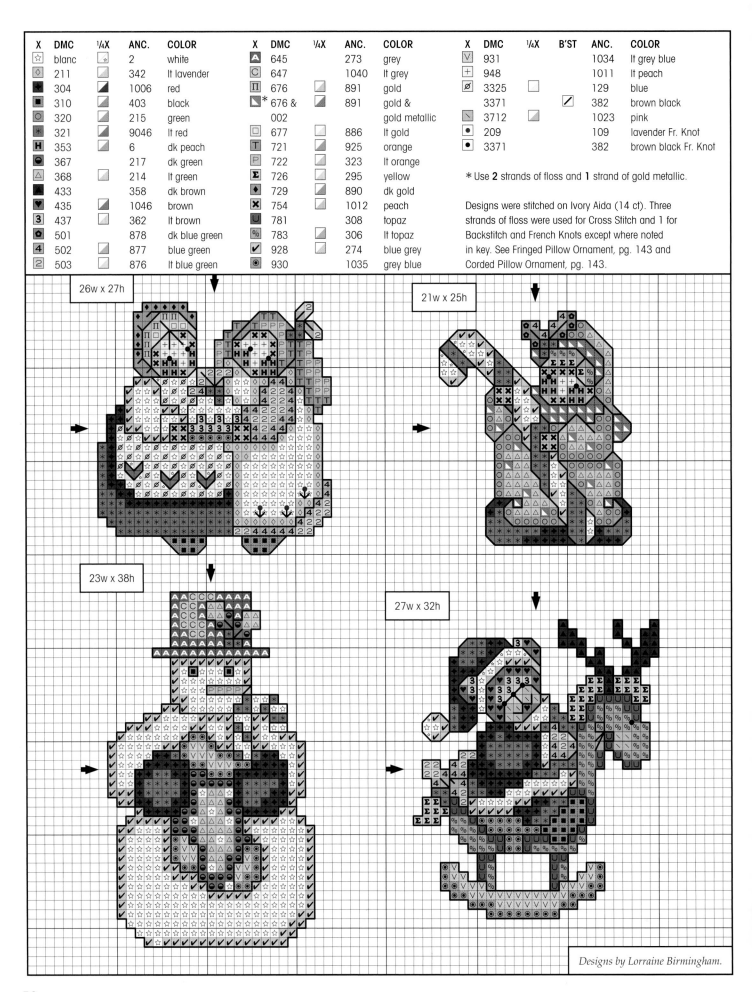

26w x 27h

21w x 25h

23w x 38h

27w x 32h

Designs by Lorraine Birmingham.

52

X	DMC	1/4X	ANC.	COLOR	X	DMC	1/4X	B'ST	ANC.	COLOR	X	DMC	1/4X	B'ST	ANC.	COLOR
☆	blanc		2	white	2	503			876	lt blue green	⊟	3078			292	lt yellow
⊠	209		109	lavender	◨*	676 &		/	891	gold &	⌀	3325			129	lt blue
♡	210		108	lt lavender		002				gold metallic		3371		/	382	brown black
◆	304		1006	red	T	721			925	orange	↘	3712			1023	pink
◼	310		403	black	P	722			323	lt orange	Π	3755			140	blue
◎	320		215	green	✤	725			305	dk yellow	●	3371			382	brown black Fr. Knot
✳	321		9046	lt red	◇	727			293	yellow						
H	353		6	dk peach	✕	754			1012	peach						
△	368		214	lt green	A	927			848	blue grey						
✿	434		310	dk brown	✔	928			274	lt blue grey						
♥	435		1046	brown	◉	930			1035	grey blue						
3	437		362	lt brown	V	931			1034	lt grey blue						
4	502		877	blue green	+	948			1011	lt peach						

*Use **2** strands of floss and **1** strand of metallic.

Designs were stitched on Ivory Aida (14 ct).
Three strands of floss were used for Cross
Stitch and 1 for Backstitch and French Knots
except where noted in key. See Fringed Pillow
Ornament, pg. 143.

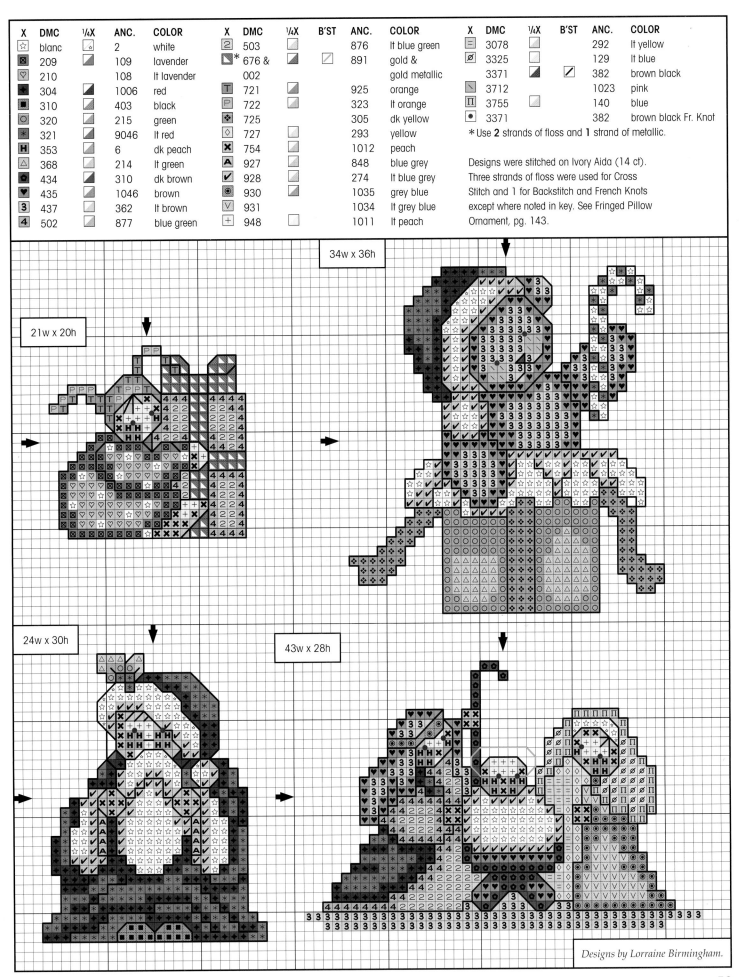

34w x 36h

21w x 20h

24w x 30h

43w x 28h

Designs by Lorraine Birmingham.

53

Christmas Cubbies

Clad in footed flannel pj's, three "beary" excited cubs busily prepare for Christmas. Fashioned into pillow ornaments, they're sure to be a joy!

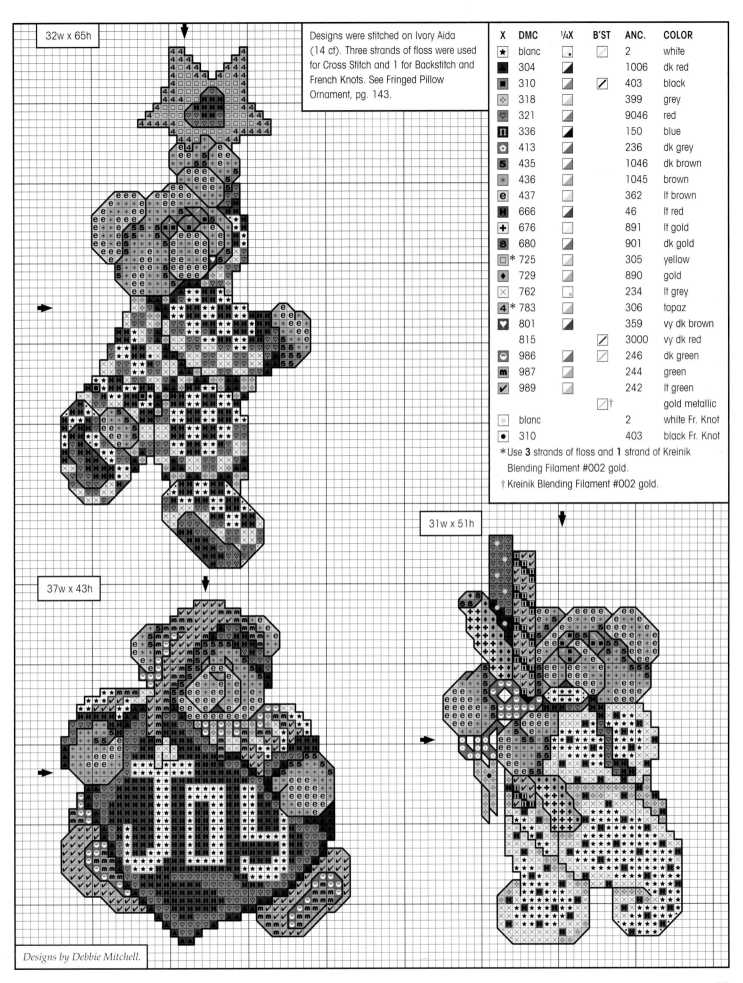

32w x 65h

Designs were stitched on Ivory Aida (14 ct). Three strands of floss were used for Cross Stitch and 1 for Backstitch and French Knots. See Fringed Pillow Ornament, pg. 143.

X	DMC	1/4X	B'ST	ANC.	COLOR
★	blanc			2	white
■	304			1006	dk red
■	310		/	403	black
◇	318			399	grey
♥	321			9046	red
Π	336			150	blue
✿	413			236	dk grey
5	435			1046	dk brown
*	436			1045	brown
e	437			362	lt brown
H	666			46	lt red
+	676			891	lt gold
8	680			901	dk gold
□*	725			305	yellow
◆	729			890	gold
⊠	762			234	lt grey
4*	783			306	topaz
♥	801			359	vy dk brown
	815		/	3000	vy dk red
◔	986			246	dk green
m	987			244	green
✔	989			242	lt green
			/†		gold metallic
◉	blanc			2	white Fr. Knot
●	310			403	black Fr. Knot

*Use **3** strands of floss and 1 strand of Kreinik Blending Filament #002 gold.

† Kreinik Blending Filament #002 gold.

37w x 43h

31w x 51h

Designs by Debbie Mitchell.

55

Mitten Merriment

Warm up your evergreen with these merry mittens! Sure to make the season bright,
each little pair features cute Christmasy cuffs sprinkled with whimsical stitches.

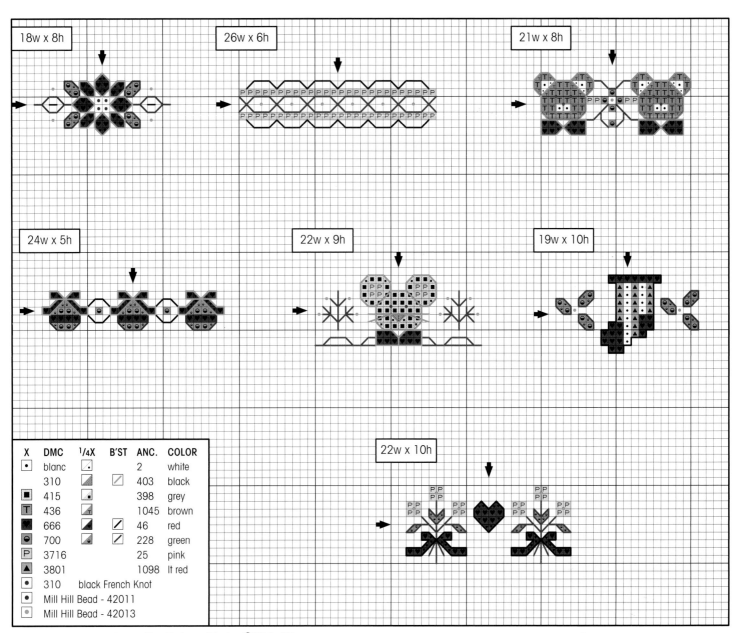

X	DMC	¼X	B'ST	ANC.	COLOR
•	blanc			2	white
	310		✓	403	black
■	415			398	grey
T	436			1045	brown
	666		✓	46	red
◐	700		✓	228	green
P	3716			25	pink
▲	3801			1098	lt red
•	310		black French Knot		
•	Mill Hill Bead - 42011				
◦	Mill Hill Bead - 42013				

Each design was stitched on an 8" x 4" piece of Zweigart® White Aida (14 ct). Two strands of floss were used for Cross Stitch and 1 for Backstitch and French Knots. Attach beads using 1 strand of DMC 666 floss for red beads and 1 strand of DMC blanc floss for gold beads. They were made into ornaments.

For each ornament, you will need two 5" squares of fabric for mitten, tracing paper, pencil, and a fabric marking pencil.

Centering design horizontally, trim stitched piece to measure 5¹/₂" x 2¹/₄".

For mitten cuff, turn short edges of stitched piece ¹/₂" to wrong side; press. Matching right sides and long edges; fold stitched piece in half. Using a ¹/₄" seam allowance, sew long edges together; trim seam allowance and turn stitched piece right side out. With seam centered in back, press stitched piece flat.

For mitten pattern, trace pattern onto tracing paper; cut out pattern. Position pattern on wrong side of one fabric piece; pin pattern in place. Use fabric marking pencil to draw around pattern; remove pattern. Matching right sides and raw edges, pin mitten fabric pieces together.

For mitten, leave top edge open and use a short stitch length to sew directly on drawn line. Trim top edge along drawn line and trim seam allowance to ¹/₄"; clip curves and turn mitten right side out. Press top edge of mitten ¹/₂" to wrong side.

Referring to photo, wrap cuff around top of mitten; pin in place. Blind stitch short ends of cuff together. Tack cuff to mitten at side seams.

Designs by Ann Townsend.

Homespun Angels

Our little country cherubs want to bless your holiday season! Bearing gifts of stars, hearts, and even a hearty treat, these homespun angel ornaments are reminders of the joy that comes with Christmas giving.

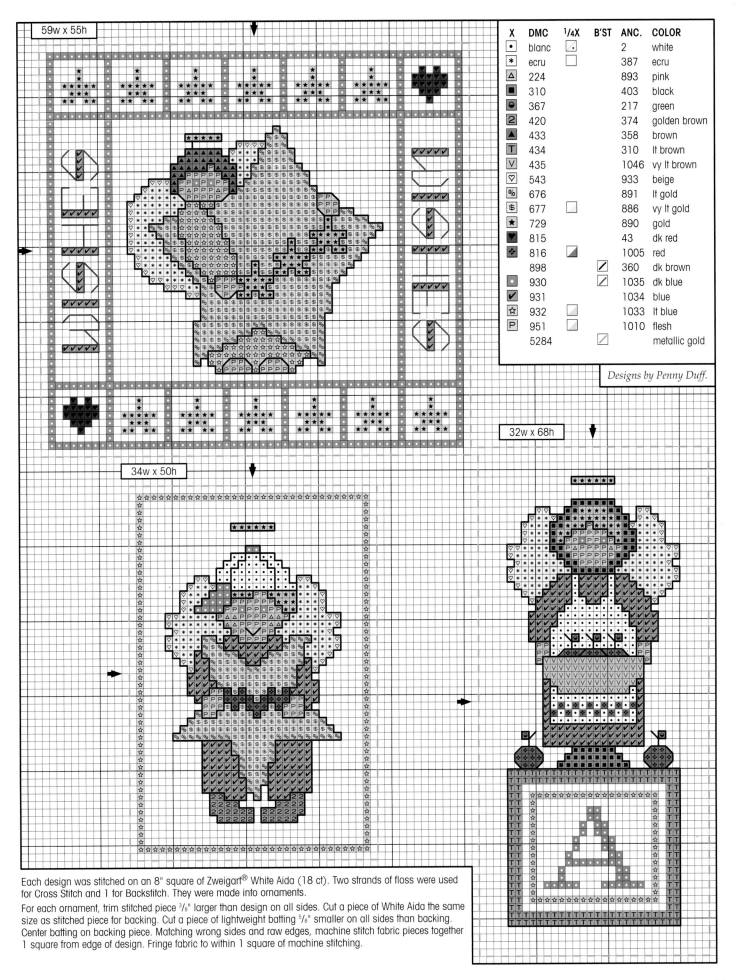

X	DMC	1/4X	B'ST	ANC.	COLOR
•	blanc			2	white
*	ecru			387	ecru
△	224			893	pink
■	310			403	black
⊖	367			217	green
2	420			374	golden brown
▲	433			358	brown
T	434			310	lt brown
V	435			1046	vy lt brown
♡	543			933	beige
%	676			891	lt gold
$	677			886	vy lt gold
★	729			890	gold
♥	815			43	dk red
✤	816			1005	red
	898		✓	360	dk brown
▢	930		✓	1035	dk blue
✔	931			1034	blue
☆	932			1033	lt blue
P	951			1010	flesh
	5284		✓		metallic gold

Designs by Penny Duff.

59w x 55h

34w x 50h

32w x 68h

Each design was stitched on an 8" square of Zweigart® White Aida (18 ct). Two strands of floss were used for Cross Stitch and 1 for Backstitch. They were made into ornaments.

For each ornament, trim stitched piece ³/₈" larger than design on all sides. Cut a piece of White Aida the same size as stitched piece for backing. Cut a piece of lightweight batting ⁵/₈" smaller on all sides than backing. Center batting on backing piece. Matching wrong sides and raw edges, machine stitch fabric pieces together 1 square from edge of design. Fringe fabric to within 1 square of machine stitching.

Festive fashions

There's nothing like festive fashion wear to put you in the Christmas spirit, so we've gathered a collection of our favorites for the whole family. Worked over waste canvas, the designs go on lots of wearables, from sweatshirts, cotton shirts, and denims to sock cuffs. What a fun and inexpensive way to build your family's seasonal attire.

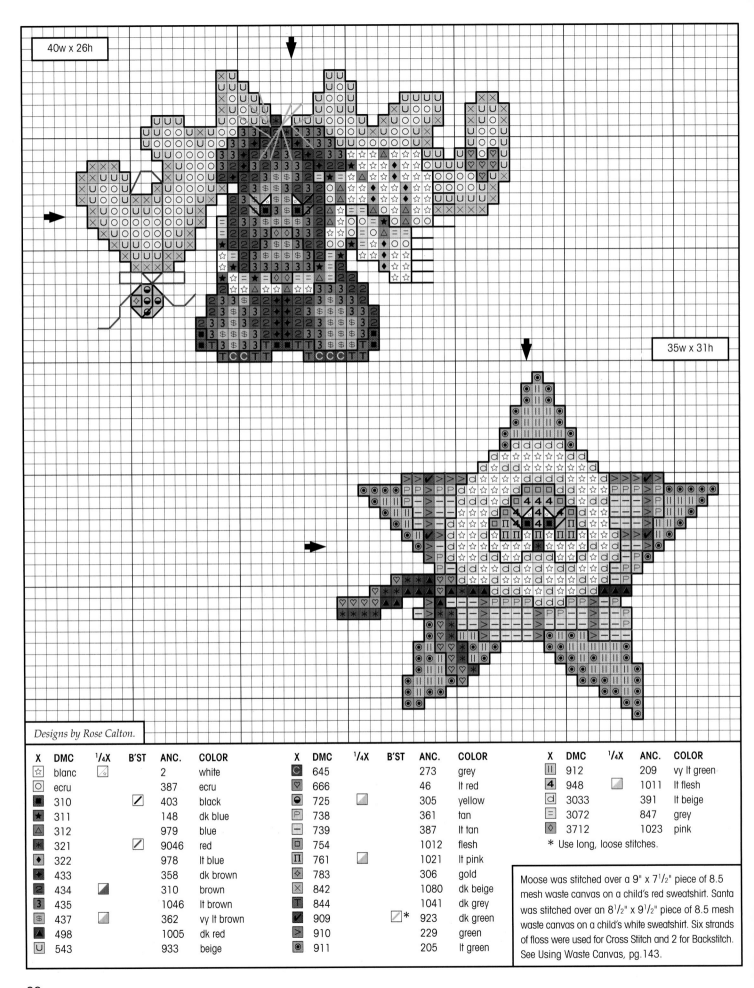

40w x 26h

35w x 31h

Designs by Rose Calton.

X	DMC	¹/₄X	B'ST	ANC.	COLOR
☆	blanc	◸		2	white
○	ecru			387	ecru
■	310		╱	403	black
★	311			148	dk blue
△	312			979	blue
✳	321		╱	9046	red
◆	322			978	lt blue
★	433			358	dk brown
2	434	◩		310	brown
3	435			1046	lt brown
$	437	◪		362	vy lt brown
▲	498			1005	dk red
U	543			933	beige

X	DMC	¹/₄X	B'ST	ANC.	COLOR
C	645			273	grey
♥	666			46	lt red
◙	725	◪		305	yellow
P	738			361	tan
—	739			387	lt tan
▣	754			1012	flesh
Π	761	◪		1021	lt pink
✧	783			306	gold
✕	842			1080	dk beige
T	844			1041	dk grey
✔	909		╱*	923	dk green
>	910			229	green
◉	911			205	lt green

X	DMC	¹/₄X	ANC.	COLOR
‖	912		209	vy lt green
4	948	◪	1011	lt flesh
d	3033		391	lt beige
=	3072		847	grey
◇	3712		1023	pink

* Use long, loose stitches.

Moose was stitched over a 9" x 7¹/₂" piece of 8.5 mesh waste canvas on a child's red sweatshirt. Santa was stitched over an 8¹/₂" x 9¹/₂" piece of 8.5 mesh waste canvas on a child's white sweatshirt. Six strands of floss were used for Cross Stitch and 2 for Backstitch. See Using Waste Canvas, pg.143.

Buttoned-Up Santa

Slip into this merry sweatshirt and everyone will know you believe in Santa! Add dimension to his beard with buttons from your cherished collection.

X	DMC	B'ST	ANC.	COLOR
•	blanc		2	white
★	310	╱	403	black
✳	321		9046	red
>	353		6	lt coral
◼	498		1005	dk red
▼	613		831	dk tan
◈	666		46	lt red
○	712		926	vy lt tan
✕	738		361	tan
◻	739		387	lt tan
▼	754		1012	peach
◇	758		868	dk peach
=	760		1022	pink
+	761		1021	lt pink
╲	948		1011	lt peach
✿	3712		1023	dk pink

54w x 48h

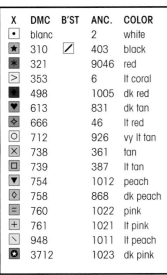

The design was stitched over a 14" x 12" piece of 6.5 mesh waste canvas on a purchased sweatshirt. Nine strands of floss were used for Cross Stitch and 3 for Backstitch. After removing waste canvas, refer to photo for placement and sew buttons to shirt. See Using Waste Canvas, pg. 143.

Design by Kathie Rueger.
Needlework adaptation by Jane Chandler.

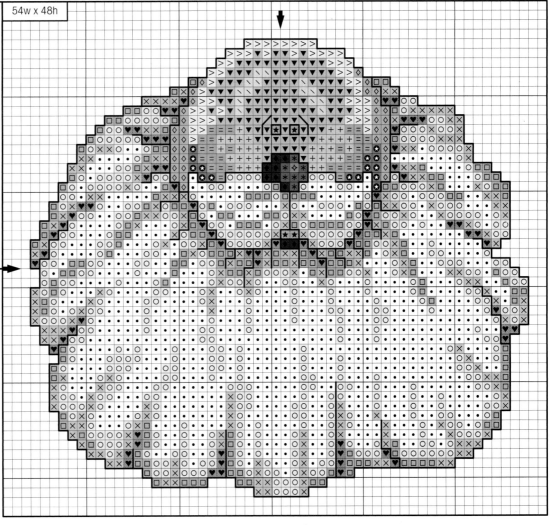

Ho Ho Ho Snowman

This jolly snowman is ho-ho-hoping you'll have a happy holiday season! Enhanced with "snowflake" beads and playfully fringed accessories, he makes this sweatshirt a festive way to celebrate Christmas.

84w x 74h

X	DMC	¼X	B'ST	ANC.	COLOR
☆	blanc	◪	⟋	2	white
■	310		⟋	403	black
✕	436			1045	tan
◉	666			46	red
5	700			228	dk green
★	701			227	green
▽	725		⟋*	305	lt gold
2	782			307	dk gold
◎	783			306	gold
	797		⟋	132	dk blue
◈	817			13	dk red
✳	900	◩	⟋	333	dk orange
✧	947			330	orange
◒	3753			1031	blue
+	3756			1037	lt blue
●	Mill Hill Glass Seed Beads #00479 white				
●	Indicates placement of dk red fringe				
●	Indicates placement of lt gold fringe				
✻ Work in long stitches using 6 strands.					

Design was stitched over a 13" x 12" piece of 10 mesh waste canvas on a purchased sweatshirt. Five strands of floss were used for Cross Stitch and 2 for Backstitch. See Using Waste Canvas, pg. 143.

For fringe, refer to chart for floss color and placement and thread a needle with a 6" length of 6 strand floss. Insert needle from right side to wrong side of shirt leaving 3" of floss on right side; insert needle back through to right side of shirt close to entry point. Remove needle; place ends of floss together and tie in an overhand knot, using point of needle to guide knot as close to shirt as possible. Trim ends as desired.

Bead placement is shown on the chart by a black dot. To sew bead in place, use sewing thread and a fine needle that will pass through bead. Secure thread on back of fabric. Bring needle up at dot, run needle through bead then down through fabric. Secure thread on back or move to next bead.

Design by Vicky Howard.

Reindeer Fun

Our rosy-cheeked reindeer, with his bright red nose, looks just like the sort to be guiding Santa's sleigh to your rooftop. Wear him to a Christmas party, and he'll guide you through an evening of holiday fun.

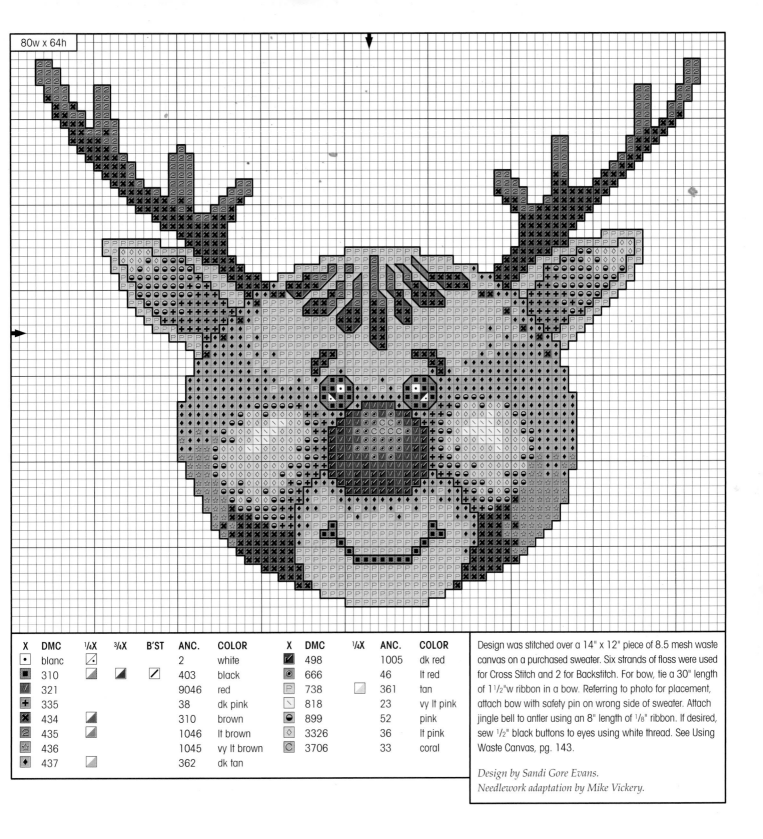

X	DMC	¼X	¾X	B'ST	ANC.	COLOR		X	DMC	¼X	ANC.	COLOR
•	blanc				2	white			498		1005	dk red
■	310				403	black		◉	666		46	lt red
☑	321				9046	red		P	738		361	tan
+	335				38	dk pink		╲	818		23	vy lt pink
✕	434				310	brown		◓	899		52	pink
2	435				1046	lt brown		◇	3326		36	lt pink
☆	436				1045	vy lt brown		C	3706		33	coral
◆	437				362	dk tan						

Design was stitched over a 14" x 12" piece of 8.5 mesh waste canvas on a purchased sweater. Six strands of floss were used for Cross Stitch and 2 for Backstitch. For bow, tie a 30" length of 1½"w ribbon in a bow. Referring to photo for placement, attach bow with safety pin on wrong side of sweater. Attach jingle bell to antler using an 8" length of ⅛" ribbon. If desired, sew ½" black buttons to eyes using white thread. See Using Waste Canvas, pg. 143.

Design by Sandi Gore Evans.
Needlework adaptation by Mike Vickery.

80w x 64h

Pretty Pockets

Add one of these quick-to-stitch designs to the pocket of a plain cotton shirt and your gift-giving is all wrapped up! Be sure to include a note permitting it to be opened before Christmas.

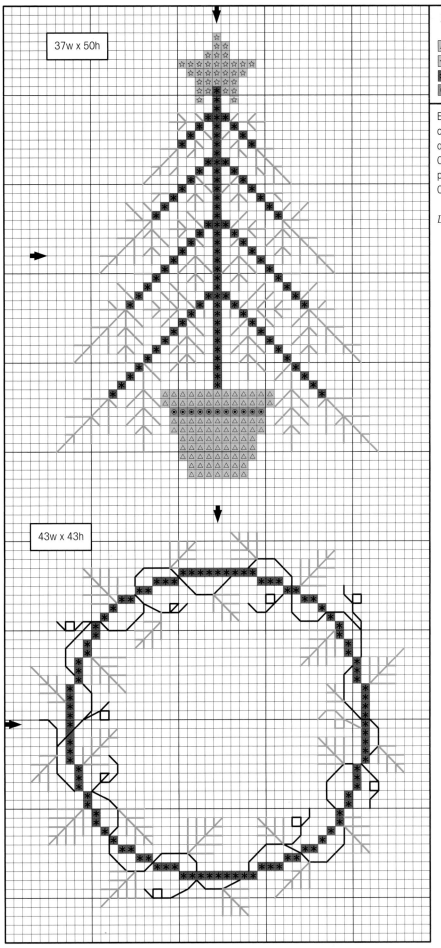

X	DMC	B'ST	ANC.	COLOR
	319	◹	218	green
△	648		900	grey
☆	725		305	yellow
✳	801	◹	359	brown
◉	931		1034	blue

37w x 50h

43w x 43h

Each design was stitched over a 5" square of 14 mesh waste canvas on the pocket of a shirt. Three strands of floss were used for Cross Stitch and 2 for Backstitch. Refer to photo for button placement. See Using Waste Canvas, pg. 143.

Designs by Jane Chandler.

Woodland Wearable

A natural choice for an outdoors enthusiast, this woodland border has a simplistic styling that's a breeze to finish. Doesn't it look great stitched on a sweatshirt in warm earth tones?

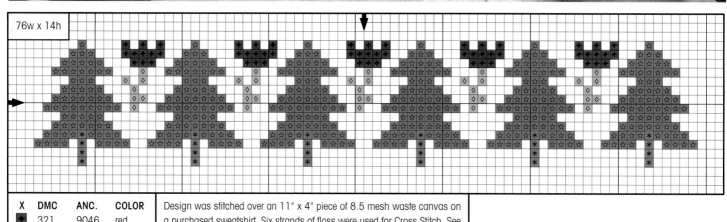

76w x 14h

X	DMC	ANC.	COLOR
+	321	9046	red
◇	368	214	lt green
*	435	1046	brown
☆	699	923	green

Design was stitched over an 11" x 4" piece of 8.5 mesh waste canvas on a purchased sweatshirt. Six strands of floss were used for Cross Stitch. See Using Waste Canvas, pg. 143.

Design by Polly Carbonari.

Peekaboo Santa

This elfish Santa, dressed in a brilliant red robe, looks darling stitched on chambray. Peeking over the top of your pocket, he offers a playful way to spread the joy of Christmas.

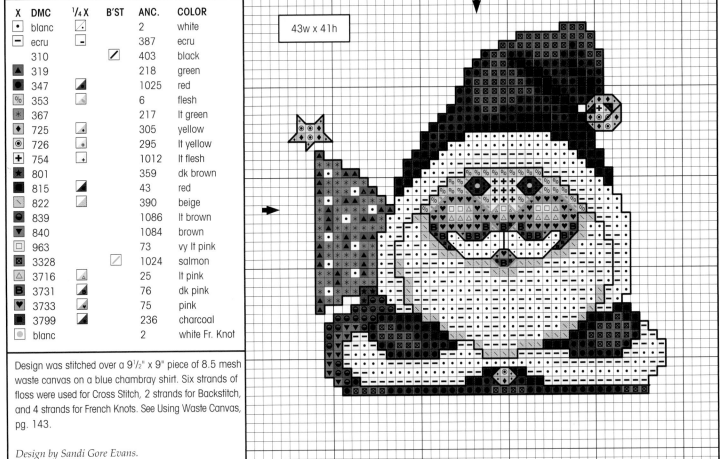

X	DMC	¼ X	B'ST	ANC.	COLOR
•	blanc	◢		2	white
–	ecru	–		387	ecru
	310		◿	403	black
▲	319			218	green
◕	347	◢		1025	red
%	353	◢		6	flesh
✳	367			217	lt green
◆	725	◢		305	yellow
◉	726	◢		295	lt yellow
+	754	+		1012	lt flesh
★	801			359	dk brown
■	815	◢		43	red
◺	822	◢		390	beige
⬤	839			1086	lt brown
▼	840			1084	brown
▫	963			73	vy lt pink
⊠	3328		◿	1024	salmon
△	3716	◢		25	lt pink
B	3731	◢		76	dk pink
♥	3733	◢		75	pink
■	3799	◢		236	charcoal
◉	blanc			2	white Fr. Knot

43w x 41h

Design was stitched over a 9½" x 9" piece of 8.5 mesh waste canvas on a blue chambray shirt. Six strands of floss were used for Cross Stitch, 2 strands for Backstitch, and 4 strands for French Knots. See Using Waste Canvas, pg. 143.

Design by Sandi Gore Evans.

Cheery Cuffs

Our cozy socks will keep your feet warm and toasty all through the holidays. Adorned with festive Christmas motifs, they're perfect accessories for your seasonal attire.

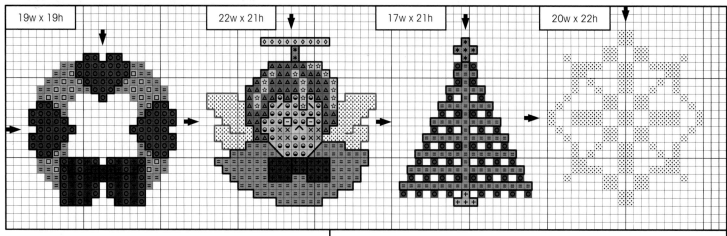

Each design was stitched on the cuff of a purchased sock over a 3" square of 14 mesh waste canvas. Three strands of floss were used for Cross Stitch and 1 for Backstitch. See Using Waste Canvas, pg. 143.

Designs by Maryanne Moreck and Terrie Lee Steinmeyer. ©1996

X	DMC	B'ST	ANC.	COLOR	X	DMC	¼X	B'ST	ANC.	COLOR
⊡	blanc		2	white	✳	725			305	dk yellow
	304	⟋	1006	dk red	◇	726			295	yellow
−	312		979	dk blue	◔	754	◪		1012	peach
◎	321		9046	red	=	986	◪		246	green
+	322	⟋	978	blue	▢	987			244	lt green
▲	435		1046	brown	✕	3326			36	pink
☆	436		1045	lt brown		3371		⟋	382	dk brown
✚	666		46	dk red						

Friendly Faces

Wear one of these festive fellows to your next holiday gathering and you're sure to spread lots of cheer — and get plenty of hugs!

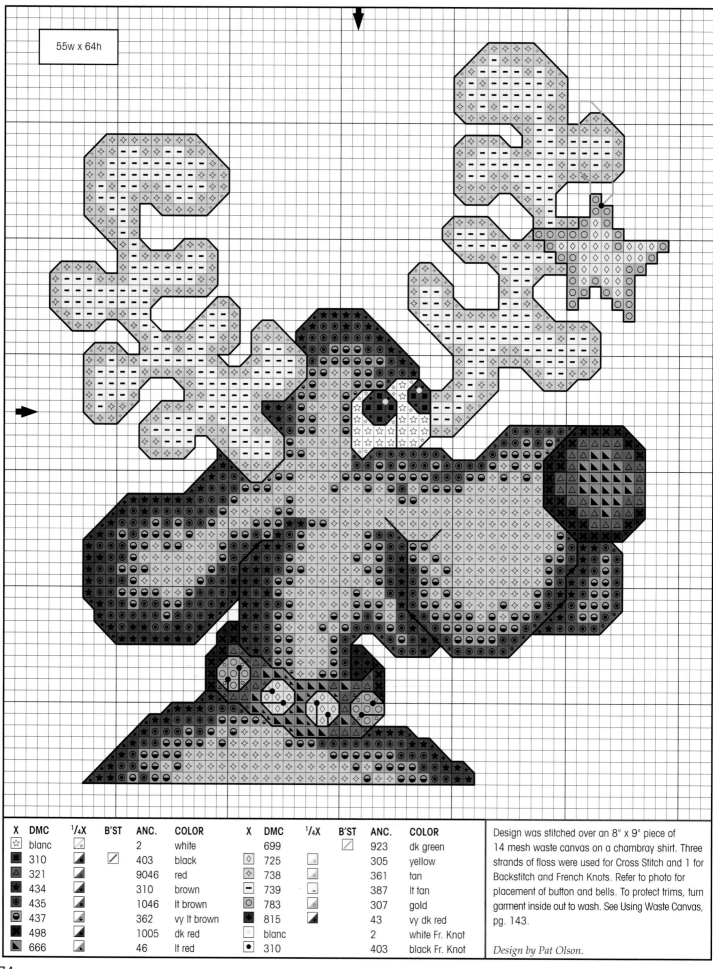

55w x 64h

X	DMC	¼X	B'ST	ANC.	COLOR	X	DMC	¼X	B'ST	ANC.	COLOR
☆	blanc			2	white		699			923	dk green
■	310			403	black	◇	725			305	yellow
▲	321			9046	red	✦	738			361	tan
◉	434			310	brown	−	739			387	lt tan
◐	435			1046	lt brown	◎	783			307	gold
◒	437			362	vy lt brown	✦	815			43	vy dk red
◼	498			1005	dk red		blanc			2	white Fr. Knot
◣	666			46	lt red	●	310			403	black Fr. Knot

Design was stitched over an 8" x 9" piece of 14 mesh waste canvas on a chambray shirt. Three strands of floss were used for Cross Stitch and 1 for Backstitch and French Knots. Refer to photo for placement of button and bells. To protect trims, turn garment inside out to wash. See Using Waste Canvas, pg. 143.

Design by Pat Olson.

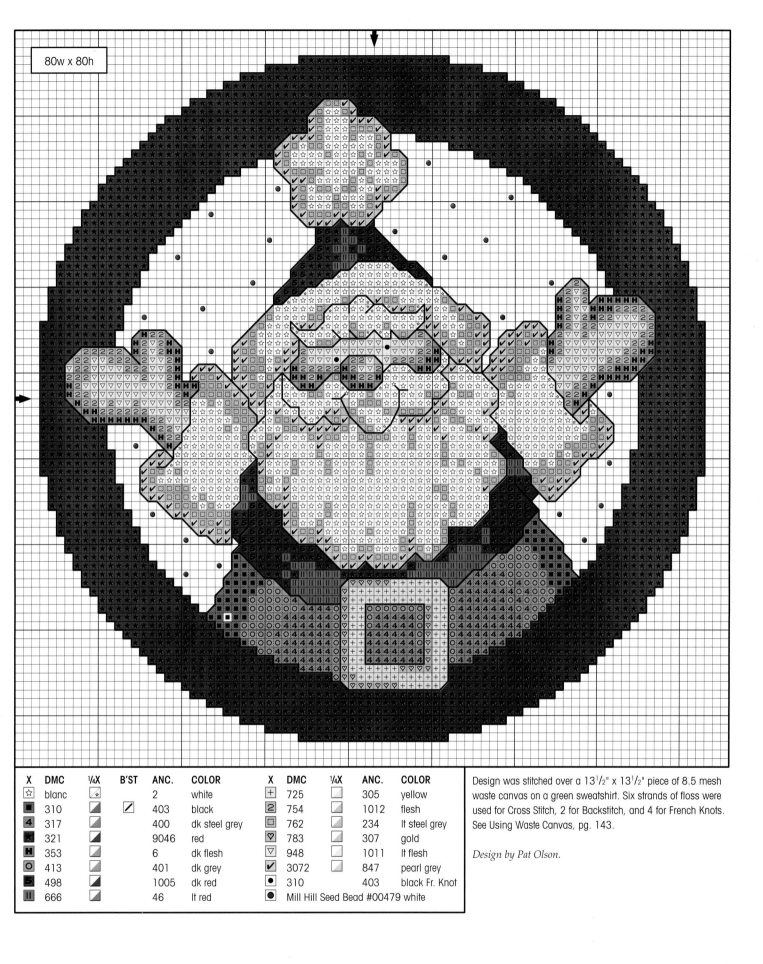

X	DMC	¼X	B'ST	ANC.	COLOR	X	DMC	¼X	ANC.	COLOR
☆	blanc	⭐		2	white	+	725		305	yellow
■	310	◪	◢	403	black	2	754		1012	flesh
4	317	◪		400	dk steel grey	□	762		234	lt steel grey
★	321	◪		9046	red	♥	783		307	gold
H	353	◪		6	dk flesh	▽	948		1011	lt flesh
O	413	◪		401	dk grey	✔	3072		847	pearl grey
5	498	◪		1005	dk red	●	310		403	black Fr. Knot
‖	666	◪		46	lt red	◉	Mill Hill Seed Bead #00479 white			

Design was stitched over a 13½" x 13½" piece of 8.5 mesh waste canvas on a green sweatshirt. Six strands of floss were used for Cross Stitch, 2 for Backstitch, and 4 for French Knots. See Using Waste Canvas, pg. 143.

Design by Pat Olson.

80w x 80h

All Through the House

Hospitality is in the details, especially during the holidays when friends and family gather to create memories that will last a lifetime. Festive little touches sprinkled throughout the house — from the front door to the bath — add to the Yuletide atmosphere. This collection of handmade holiday décor offers many wonderful ways to welcome your guests.

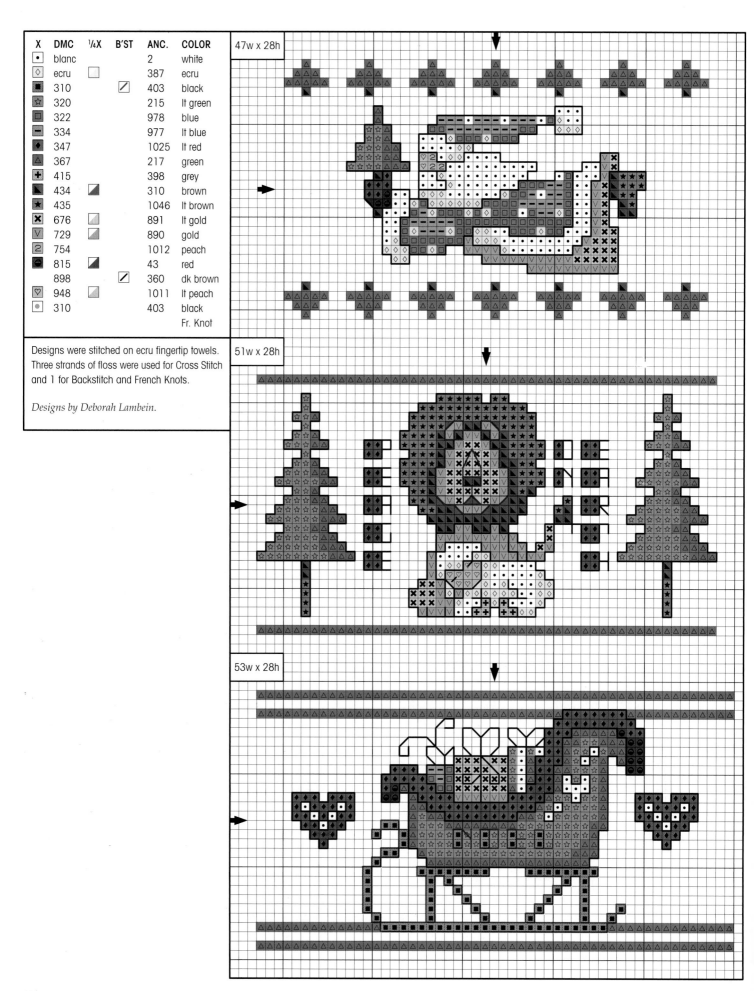

X	DMC	1/4X	B'ST	ANC.	COLOR
•	blanc			2	white
◇	ecru	☐		387	ecru
■	310		╱	403	black
☆	320			215	lt green
☐	322			978	blue
—	334			977	lt blue
◆	347			1025	lt red
△	367			217	green
✚	415			398	grey
◣	434	◤		310	brown
★	435			1046	lt brown
✖	676	◢		891	lt gold
∨	729	◢		890	gold
2	754	◢		1012	peach
◙	815	◤		43	red
	898		╱	360	dk brown
♡	948	◢		1011	lt peach
•	310			403	black
					Fr. Knot

Designs were stitched on ecru fingertip towels. Three strands of floss were used for Cross Stitch and 1 for Backstitch and French Knots.

Designs by Deborah Lambein.

47w x 28h

51w x 28h

53w x 28h

78

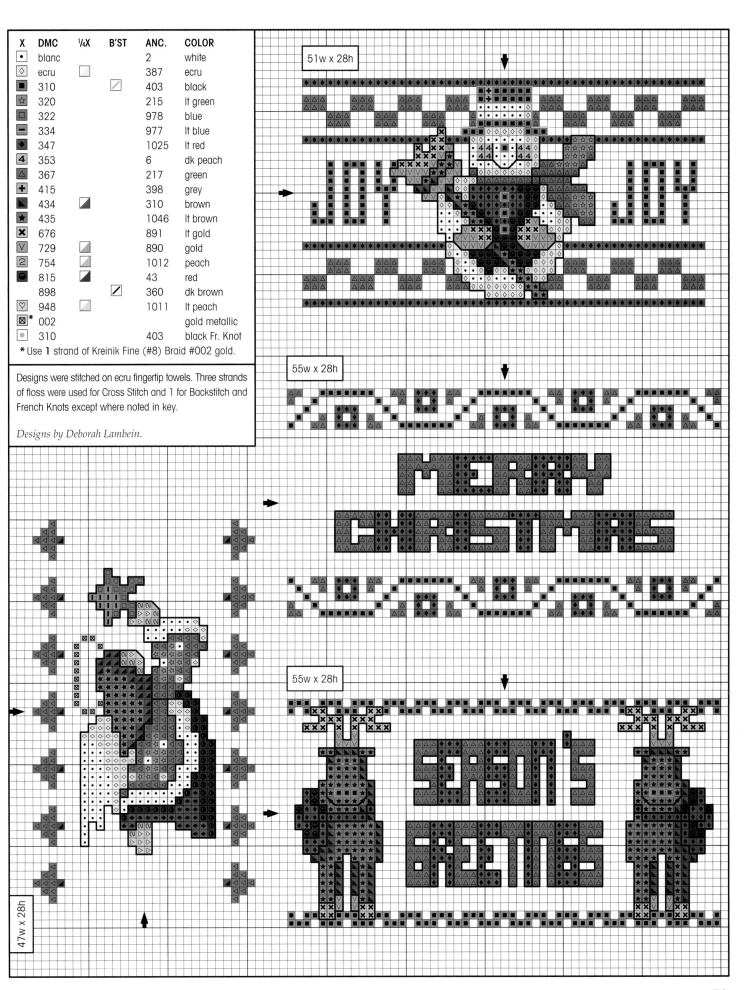

X	DMC	¼X	B'ST	ANC.	COLOR
•	blanc			2	white
◇	ecru	▢		387	ecru
■	310		◢	403	black
☆	320			215	lt green
▢	322			978	blue
−	334			977	lt blue
◆	347			1025	lt red
4	353			6	dk peach
△	367			217	green
+	415			398	grey
◣	434	◿		310	brown
★	435			1046	lt brown
✕	676			891	lt gold
∨	729	◿		890	gold
2	754	◿		1012	peach
◓	815	◢		43	red
	898		◢	360	dk brown
♡	948	◿		1011	lt peach
⊠*	002				gold metallic
●	310			403	black Fr. Knot

* Use **1** strand of Kreinik Fine (#8) Braid #002 gold.

Designs were stitched on ecru fingertip towels. Three strands of floss were used for Cross Stitch and 1 for Backstitch and French Knots except where noted in key.

Designs by Deborah Lambein.

51w x 28h

55w x 28h

55w x 28h

47w x 28h

Christmas Tree *Sampler*

Tartan plaid fabric makes a cheery frame for this simple alphabet sampler stitched in the shape of a Christmas tree. The colorful piece will make a striking accent year after year.

72w x 95h

X	DMC	ANC.	COLOR
■	310	403	black
✦	498	1005	red
◇	890	218	green
☆	*002		gold metallic

*Use **1** strand of Kreinik Fine (#8)
Braid #002 gold.

Design was stitched on Ivory Aida (14 ct).
Three strands of floss were used for Cross
Stitch except where noted in key. See Ruffled
Pillow, pg. 144.

Design by Myra Parrott.

Country Inspirations

These holiday towels celebrate Christmas country-style! Inspired by loving hearts and quilt patterns, the designs offer bright touches of Americana for your home.

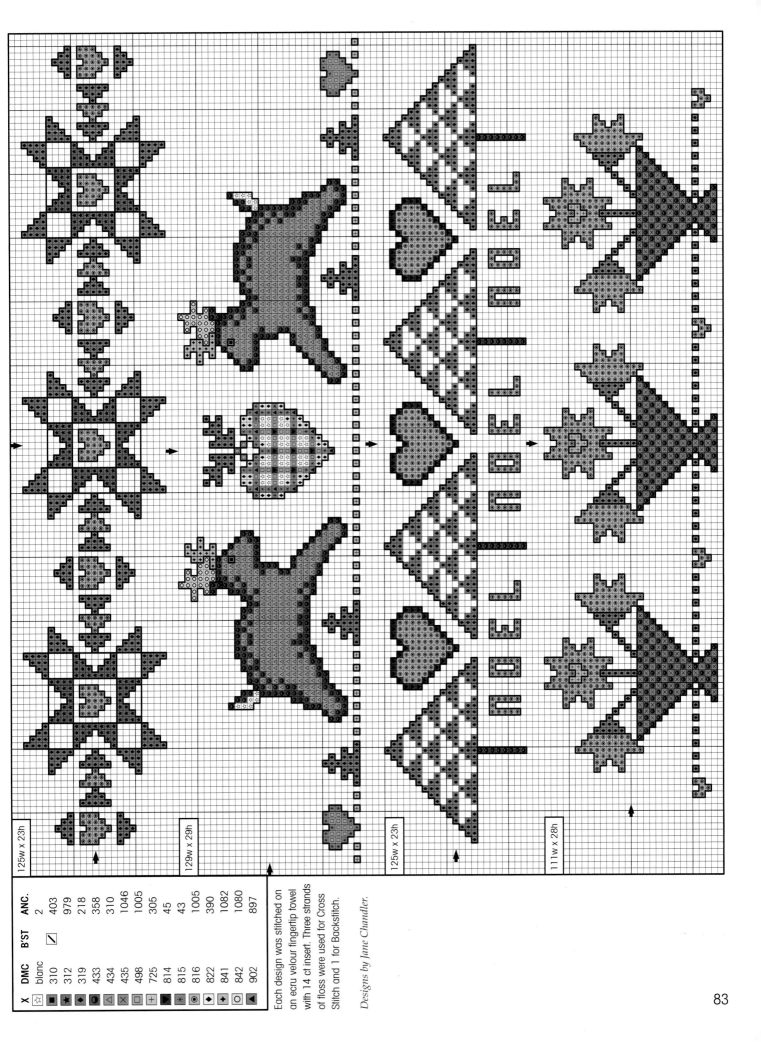

125w x 23h

129w x 29h

125w x 23h

111w x 28h

X	DMC	B'ST	ANC.
☆	blanc		2
■	310	◣	403
★	312		979
◆	319		218
◑	433		358
◁	434		310
✕	435		1046
□	498		1005
+	725		305
◼	814		45
✳	815		43
⊙	816		1005
◆	822		390
◆	841		1082
○	842		1080
◀	902		897

Each design was stitched on an ecru velour fingertip towel with 14 ct insert. Three strands of floss were used for Cross Stitch and 1 for Backstitch.

Designs by Jane Chandler.

Noel Wreath

Adorned with musical notes and the message "Noel," meaning Christmas song or ballad, this decorative wreath offers a harmonious way to greet your holiday guests.

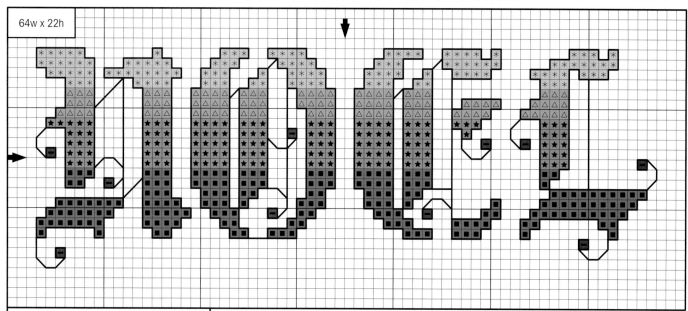

64w x 22h

X	DMC	B'ST	ANC.	COLOR
■	321		9046	red
■	911		205	dk green
★	912		209	green
	938	╱	381	brown
△	954		203	lt green
✳	955		206	vy lt green

Design was stitched on a 25" piece of White BandAida Plus™ (14 ct). Three strands of floss were used for Cross Stitch and 1 for Backstitch. It was attached to a decorated wreath.

Design by Deborah Lambein.

Santa Stop Sign

Children of all ages eagerly anticipate Santa's Yuletide visit. Our spirited door sign, featuring the lighthearted plea "Santa Stop Here," will make sure he doesn't miss your house on Christmas Eve!

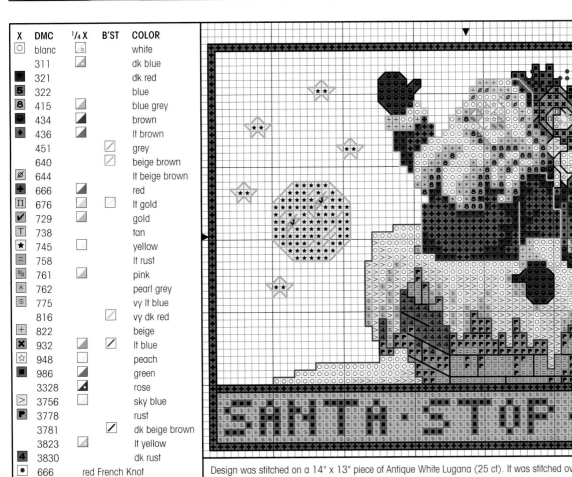

X	DMC	1/4 X	B'ST	COLOR
○	blanc			white
	311			dk blue
■	321			dk red
5	322			blue
8	415			blue grey
▣	434			brown
◆	436			lt brown
	451			grey
	640			beige brown
∅	644			lt beige brown
✚	666			red
∏	676			lt gold
✔	729			gold
T	738			tan
★	745			yellow
=	758			lt rust
%	761			pink
✳	762			pearl grey
$	775			vy lt blue
	816			vy dk red
+	822			beige
✕	932			lt blue
☆	948			peach
■	986			green
	3328			rose
>	3756			sky blue
P	3778			rust
	3781			dk beige brown
	3823			lt yellow
4	3830			dk rust
●	666			red French Knot
●	3781			dk beige brown French Knot

73w x 56h

Design was stitched on a 14" x 13" piece of Antique White Lugana (25 ct). It was stitched over 2 fabric threads. Three strands of floss were used for Cross Stitch and 1 for Backstitch and French Knots. See Corded Hanging Pillow, pg. 144.

Needlework adaptation by Anne Stanton and Nancy Dockter.

Season's Greetings

Season your kitchen with this trio of Christmas towels, and you'll have the recipe for a happy holiday! The red check towels sport a host of joyous messages to spice up the Yuletide.

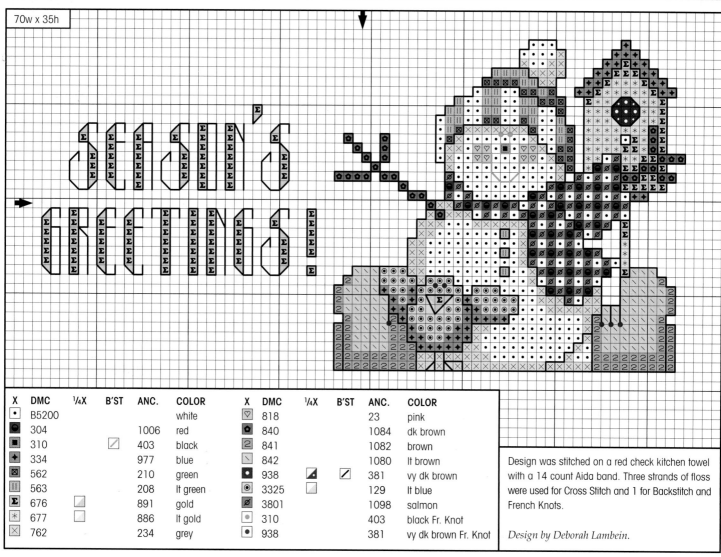

70w x 35h

X	DMC	¼X	B'ST	ANC.	COLOR	X	DMC	¼X	B'ST	ANC.	COLOR
•	B5200				white	♡	818			23	pink
◐	304			1006	red	✿	840			1084	dk brown
■	310		╱	403	black	2	841			1082	brown
✦	334			977	blue	◣	842			1080	lt brown
⊠	562			210	green	◨	938	◪	╱	381	vy dk brown
‖	563			208	lt green	◉	3325			129	lt blue
Σ	676	◹		891	gold	∅	3801			1098	salmon
*	677	◻		886	lt gold	●	310			403	black Fr. Knot
✕	762			234	grey	●	938			381	vy dk brown Fr. Knot

Design was stitched on a red check kitchen towel with a 14 count Aida band. Three strands of floss were used for Cross Stitch and 1 for Backstitch and French Knots.

Design by Deborah Lambein.

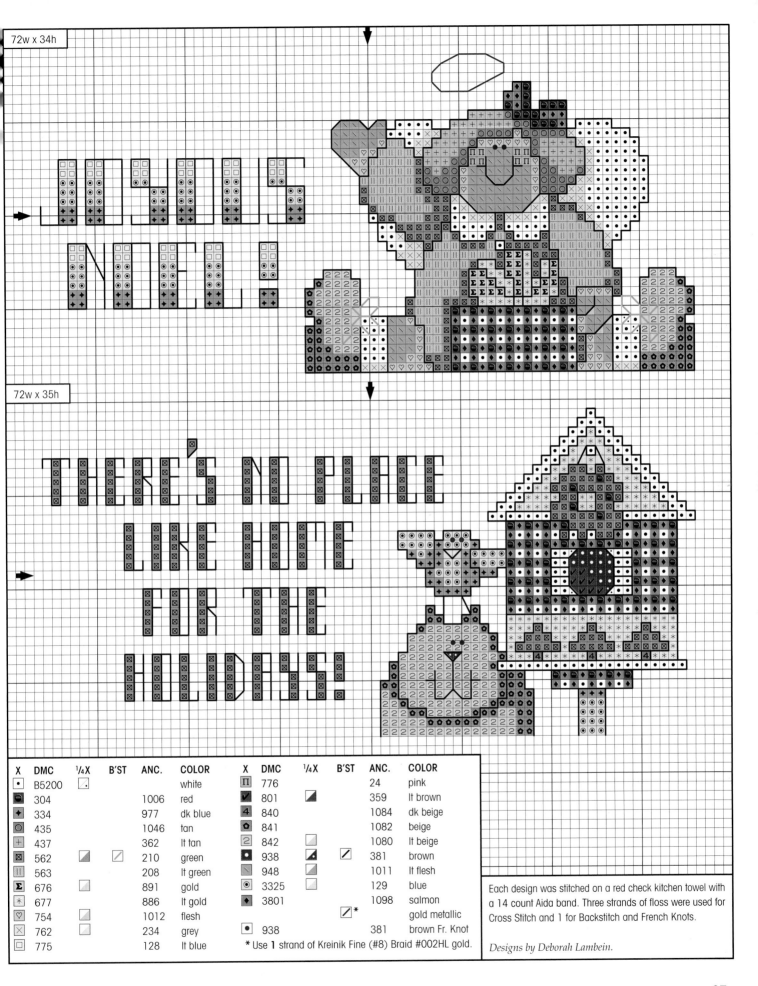

72w x 34h

72w x 35h

X	DMC	¼X	B'ST	ANC.	COLOR
•	B5200	·			white
◒	304			1006	red
✦	334			977	dk blue
◎	435			1046	tan
+	437			362	lt tan
⊠	562	◢	╱	210	green
‖	563			208	lt green
Σ	676	◢		891	gold
✳	677	◢		886	lt gold
♡	754	◢		1012	flesh
✕	762			234	grey
☐	775			128	lt blue

X	DMC	¼X	B'ST	ANC.	COLOR
Π	776			24	pink
◪	801	◢		359	lt brown
4	840			1084	dk beige
✿	841			1082	beige
2	842	◢		1080	lt beige
◙	938	◢	╱	381	brown
◩	948	◢		1011	lt flesh
◉	3325	◢		129	blue
◆	3801			1098	salmon
			╱*		gold metallic
•	938			381	brown Fr. Knot

* Use **1** strand of Kreinik Fine (#8) Braid #002HL gold.

Each design was stitched on a red check kitchen towel with a 14 count Aida band. Three strands of floss were used for Cross Stitch and 1 for Backstitch and French Knots.

Designs by Deborah Lambein.

Yuletide Linens

Set the table for a merry meal with these festive hand towels and bread cloths. Your guests will complement you on the handmade linens almost as much as on the homemade feast!

X	DMC	¼X	ANC.	COLOR	X	DMC	¼X	B'ST	ANC.	COLOR	X	DMC	ANC.	COLOR
☆	blanc		2	white	✕	762			234	grey	□	954	203	lt green
●	321		9046	red	✳	776			24	pink	❖	3072	847	beige grey
◇	666		46	lt red	★	910		◢	229	dk green				
◎	676	◢	891	gold	◉	912		◢	209	green				
+	677		886	lt gold		938		╱	381	brown				
✕	729		890	dk gold	◺	948			1011	flesh				

Designs were stitched on white fingertip towels with 14 count inserts. Three strands of floss were used for Cross Stitch and 1 for Backstitch.

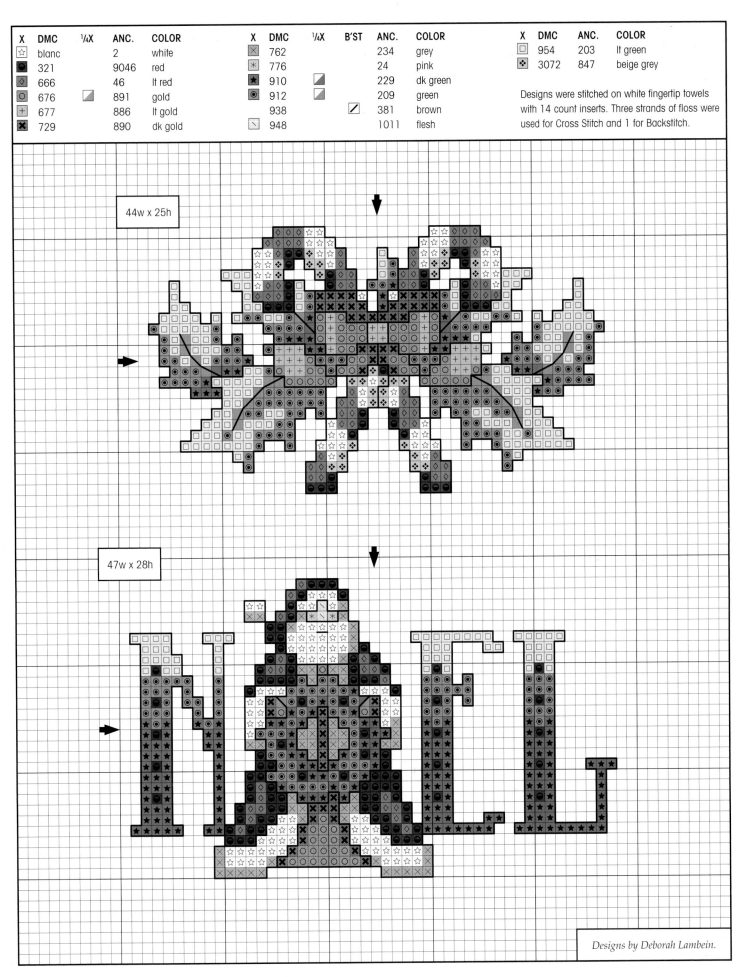

44w x 25h

47w x 28h

Designs by Deborah Lambein.

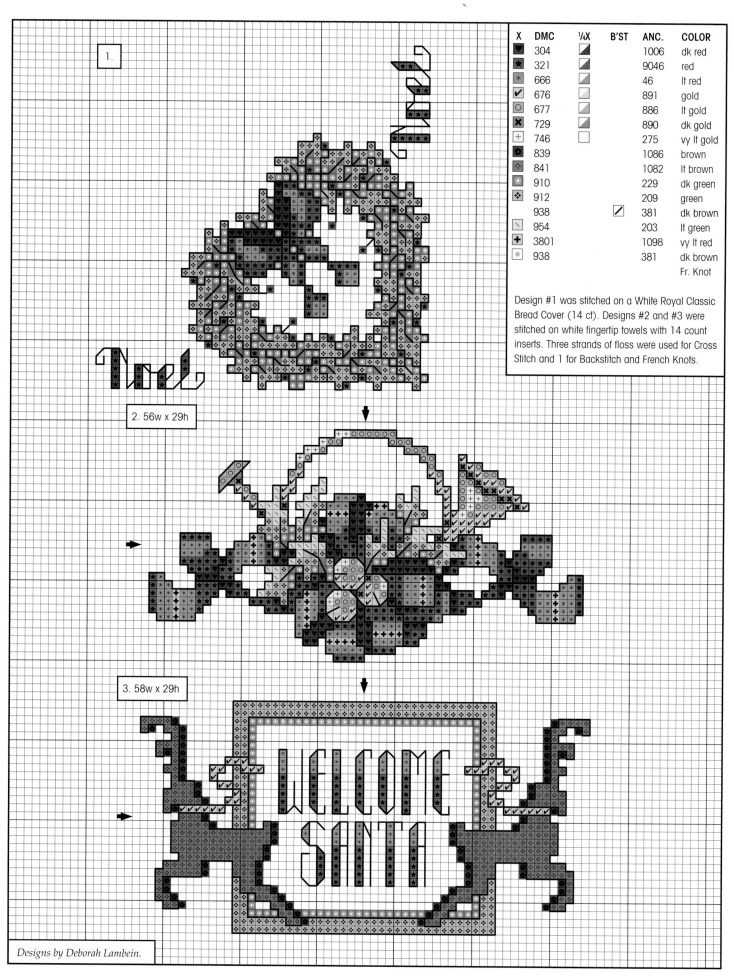

1.

X	DMC	¼X	B'ST	ANC.	COLOR
♥	304			1006	dk red
★	321			9046	red
＊	666			46	lt red
✔	676			891	gold
○	677			886	lt gold
✖	729			890	dk gold
+	746			275	vy lt gold
⬟	839			1086	brown
✦	841			1082	lt brown
◎	910			229	dk green
✤	912			209	green
	938		╱	381	dk brown
◣	954			203	lt green
✚	3801			1098	vy lt red
●	938			381	dk brown Fr. Knot

Design #1 was stitched on a White Royal Classic Bread Cover (14 ct). Designs #2 and #3 were stitched on white fingertip towels with 14 count inserts. Three strands of floss were used for Cross Stitch and 1 for Backstitch and French Knots.

2. 56w x 29h

3. 58w x 29h

Designs by Deborah Lambein.

X	DMC	¼X	B'ST	ANC.	COLOR
☆	blanc	☆		2	white
◢	304			1006	dk red
▶	321			9046	red
✻	666			46	lt red
∅	676			891	gold
+	677			886	lt gold
○	725	◹		305	yellow
✖	729			890	dk gold
▼	840			1084	brown
4	841	◺		1082	lt brown
✤	842			1080	vy lt brown
✚	910			229	dk green
◉	912			209	green
	938		╱	381	dk brown
◣	948	◿		1011	flesh
☐	954			203	lt green
C	3072			847	grey
⬠	3755	◹		140	blue
●	938			381	dk brown Fr. Knot
			╱		Kreinik Fine (#8)
					Braid #002 gold

Each design was stitched on a White Royal Classic Bread Cover (14 ct). Three strands of floss were used for Cross Stitch and 1 for Backstitch and French Knots. Designs were stitched ¾" from outer edge of fringe.

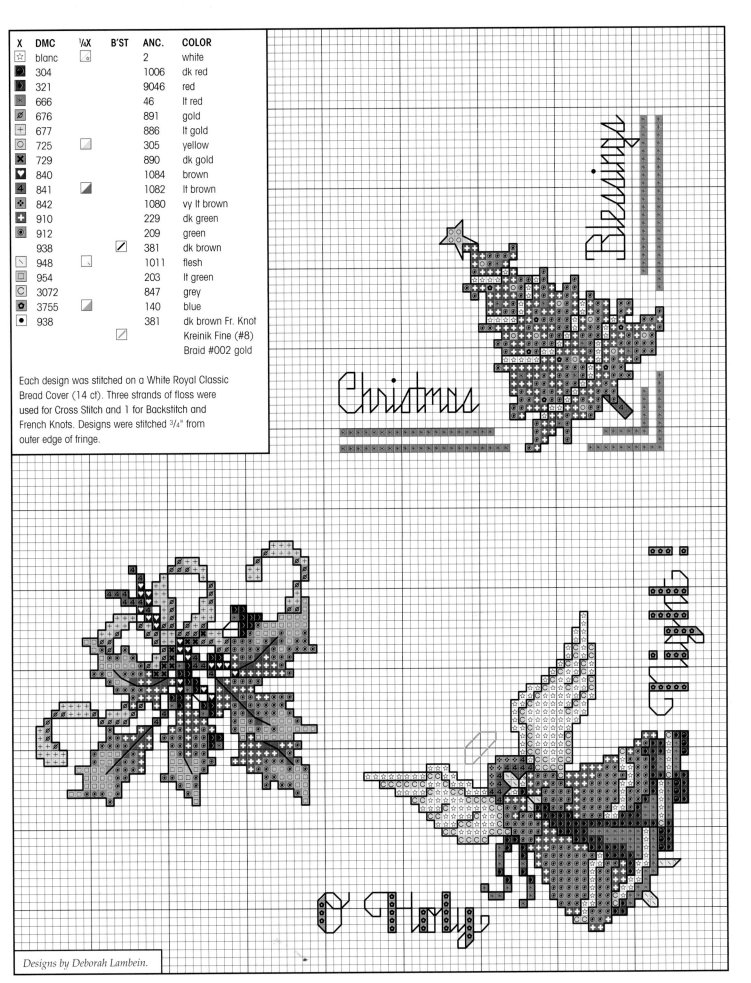

Designs by Deborah Lambein.

Winter Scenes

Pillows are ideal for spreading Christmas cheer, especially when they're embellished with winter designs like these. What an easy way to set the tone for a sentimental Yuletide season.

70w x 70h

69w x 70h

Each design was centered and stitched on an Antique White Lady Elizabeth Pillow Sham (14 ct). Three strands of floss were used for Cross Stitch and 2 for Backstitch.

Designs by Polly Carbonari.

X		DMC	ANC.	COLOR
☆		blanc	2	white
◄		ecru	387	ecru
■		310	403	black
✦		321	9046	red
✖		334	977	blue

X		DMC	ANC.	COLOR
■		433	358	brown
◈		436	1045	lt brown
◉		562	210	green
I		648	900	grey
☐		725	305	yellow

X		DMC	ANC.	COLOR
◐		738	361	tan
✹		938	381	dk brown
◉		3731	76	rose
★		3779	1012	peach

B'ST		ANC.	COLOR
◥			

93

Christmas Song

Perched on a holiday wreath, a pair of chickadees chirp a melodious Christmas song in this cheery design. The framed piece will make a sweet addition to your holiday décor.

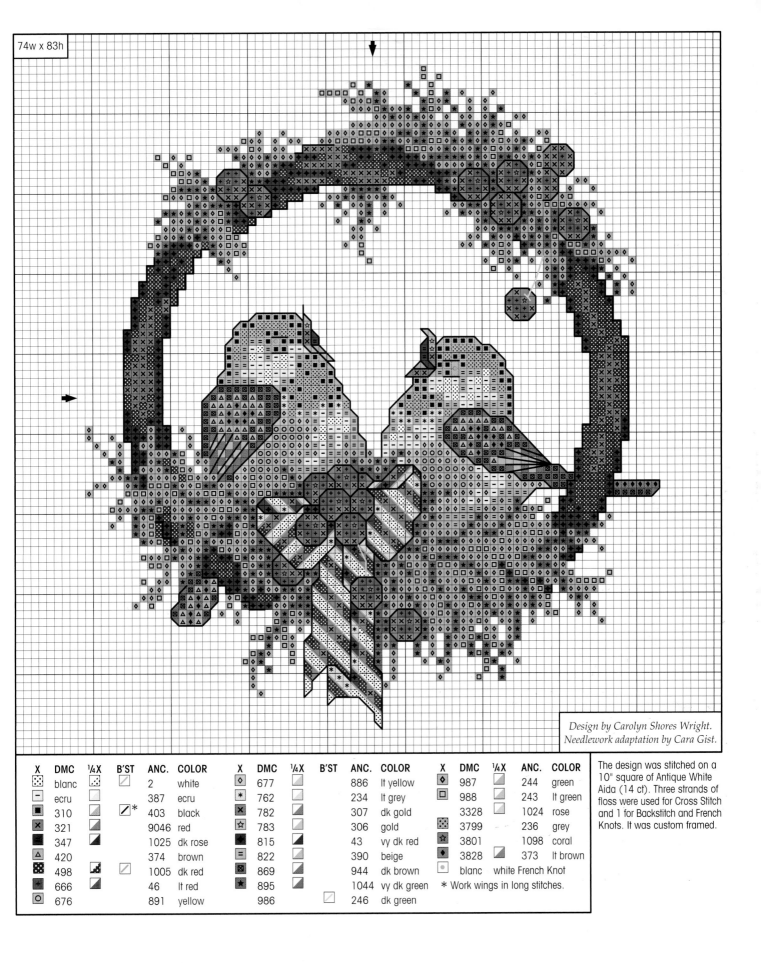

74w x 83h

Design by Carolyn Shores Wright.
Needlework adaptation by Cara Gist.

X	DMC	¼X	B'ST	ANC.	COLOR	X	DMC	¼X	B'ST	ANC.	COLOR	X	DMC	¼X	ANC.	COLOR
	blanc			2	white		677			886	lt yellow		987		244	green
	ecru			387	ecru		762			234	lt grey		988		243	lt green
	310		*	403	black		782			307	dk gold		3328		1024	rose
	321			9046	red		783			306	gold		3799		236	grey
	347			1025	dk rose		815			43	vy dk red		3801		1098	coral
	420			374	brown		822			390	beige		3828		373	lt brown
	498			1005	dk red		869			944	dk brown		blanc			white French Knot
	666			46	lt red		895			1044	vy dk green					
	676			891	yellow		986			246	dk green					

* Work wings in long stitches.

The design was stitched on a 10" square of Antique White Aida (14 ct). Three strands of floss were used for Cross Stitch and 1 for Backstitch and French Knots. It was custom framed.

Hangin' Around 'Til Christmas

You'll love having Santa "hangin' around" during the holidays on this cute towel. The whimsical design will brighten the days as you count down to Christmas.

The design was stitched on the 14 ct insert of an Ecru Velour Fingertip™ Towel.
Three strands of floss were used for Cross Stitch, 1 for Backstitch, and 2 for French Knot.

Design by Laurie Oksness.

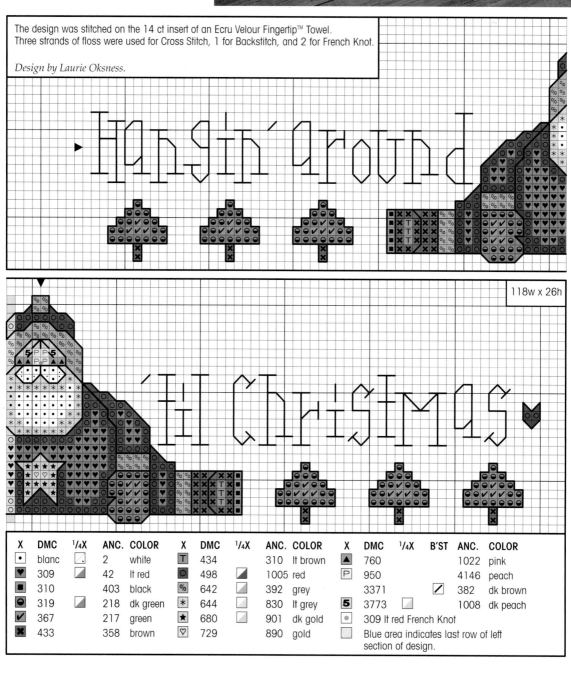

118w x 26h

X	DMC	¹/₄X	ANC.	COLOR	X	DMC	¹/₄X	ANC.	COLOR	X	DMC	¹/₄X	B'ST	ANC.	COLOR
•	blanc		2	white	T	434		310	lt brown	▲	760			1022	pink
♥	309		42	lt red	◐	498		1005	red	P	950			4146	peach
■	310		403	black	%	642		392	grey		3371		╱	382	dk brown
◉	319		218	dk green	*	644		830	lt grey	5	3773			1008	dk peach
✔	367		217	green	★	680		901	dk gold	◉	309 lt red French Knot				
✖	433		358	brown	♡	729		890	gold		Blue area indicates last row of left section of design.				

96

Bearer of Buns

All dressed up for the holidays, these sweet bears will delight your friends and family as they help you bring baked goodies to the table.

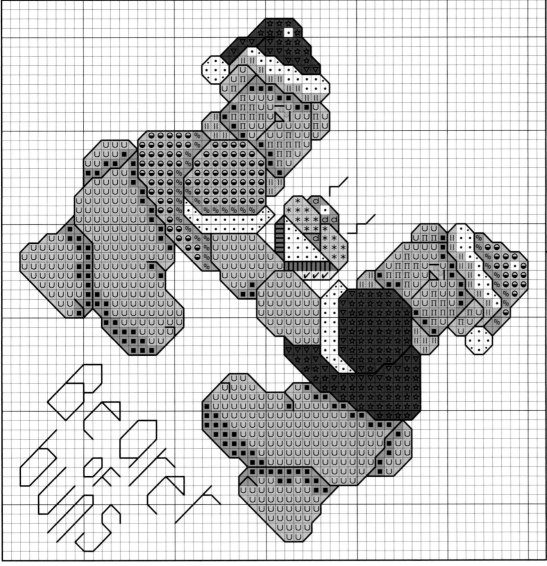

X	DMC	¼X	B'ST	ANC.
•	blanc	•		2
★	321	◥		9046
‖	415	◥		398
■	420	◥		374
U	422	◥		943
▽	498	◥		1005
◼	676	◥		891
✔	677			886
‰	699	◥		923
◒	700	◥		228
d	738	◥		361
*	739	◥		387
Π	754	◥		1012
	3371	◥	◢	382
◉	3371	French Knot		

The design was stitched in one corner of a Sal-em™ Cloth (14 ct) Breadcover, 6 squares from beginning of fringe. Three strands of floss were used for Cross Stitch and 1 for Backstitch and French Knots.

Design by Laurie Oksness.

97

Heavenly Angel

Though it's decked with shimmering ribbon and stars, this grapevine wreath gets its heavenly shine from our folk-art angel. Finished with fabric stiffener, she'll fill your home with seasonal blessings wherever she's hung.

X	DMC	1/4X	B'ST	ANC.	COLOR
★	B5200	★			white
◆	304			1006	red
✦	334			977	blue
♥	561	◢		212	dk green
‖	563	◢		208	lt green
✲	676	◢		891	gold
Π	776			24	pink
4	840			1084	beige
2	841			1082	lt beige
	938		╱	381	dk brown
╲	948	☐		1011	flesh
✔	3072	◢		847	grey
●	938			381	dk brown
					Fr. Knot
		╱			Kreinik Fine (#8)
					Braid #002HL gold

Design was stitched on White Aida (14 ct). Three strands of floss were used for Cross Stitch and 1 for Backstitch and French Knots. See Stiffened Accessory, pg. 143. Attach to a grapevine wreath.

Design by Deborah Lambein.

43w x 75h

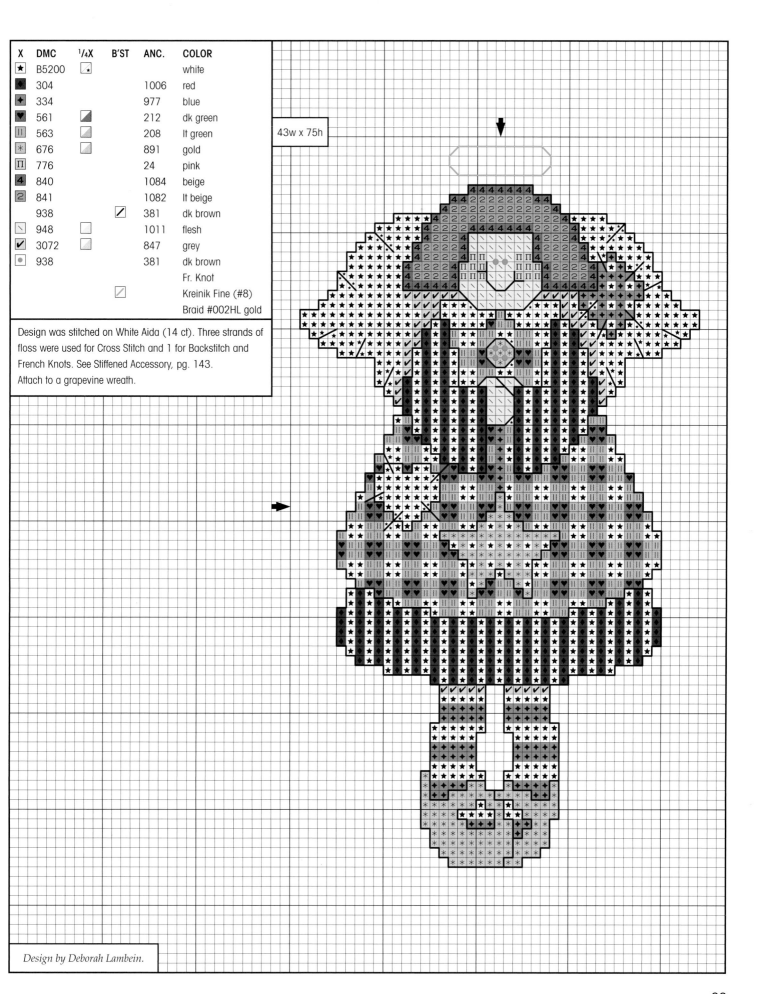

Cheery Accents

Got a notion to give your kitchen or bath a North Pole makeover this holiday? Stitch these cheery designs on hand towels for quick-and-easy accents!

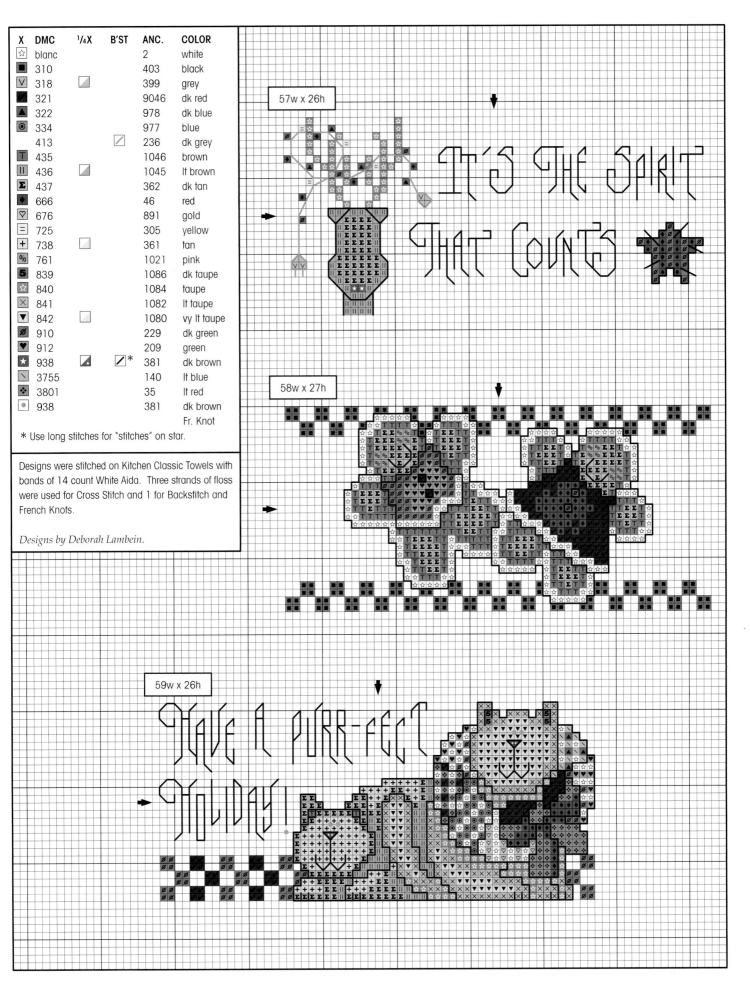

X	DMC	¼X	B'ST	ANC.	COLOR
☆	blanc			2	white
■	310			403	black
V	318	◪		399	grey
◼	321			9046	dk red
▲	322			978	dk blue
◉	334			977	blue
	413		◩	236	dk grey
T	435			1046	brown
‖	436	◪		1045	lt brown
Σ	437			362	dk tan
✦	666			46	red
♡	676			891	gold
=	725			305	yellow
+	738	◱		361	tan
%	761			1021	pink
5	839			1086	dk taupe
☆	840			1084	taupe
✕	841			1082	lt taupe
▼	842	◳		1080	vy lt taupe
∅	910			229	dk green
♥	912			209	green
★	938	◣	◩*	381	dk brown
◻	3755			140	lt blue
❖	3801			35	lt red
●	938			381	dk brown
					Fr. Knot

* Use long stitches for "stitches" on star.

Designs were stitched on Kitchen Classic Towels with bands of 14 count White Aida. Three strands of floss were used for Cross Stitch and 1 for Backstitch and French Knots.

Designs by Deborah Lambein.

57w x 26h

58w x 27h

59w x 26h

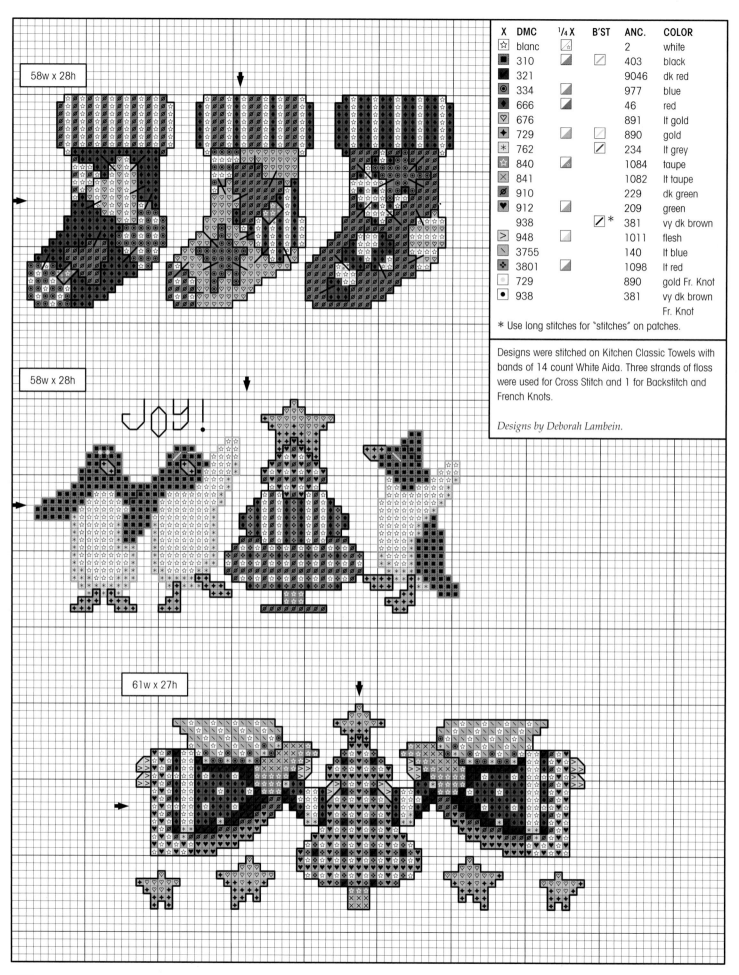

X	DMC	1/4 X	B'ST	ANC.	COLOR
☆	blanc			2	white
■	310		/	403	black
◩	321			9046	dk red
◉	334			977	blue
◆	666			46	red
♡	676			891	lt gold
✦	729			890	gold
✳	762		/	234	lt grey
☆	840			1084	taupe
✕	841			1082	lt taupe
⌀	910			229	dk green
♥	912			209	green
	938		/ *	381	vy dk brown
▷	948			1011	flesh
◢	3755			140	lt blue
❖	3801			1098	lt red
▫	729			890	gold Fr. Knot
●	938			381	vy dk brown Fr. Knot

* Use long stitches for "stitches" on patches.

Designs were stitched on Kitchen Classic Towels with bands of 14 count White Aida. Three strands of floss were used for Cross Stitch and 1 for Backstitch and French Knots.

Designs by Deborah Lambein.

58w x 28h

58w x 28h

61w x 27h

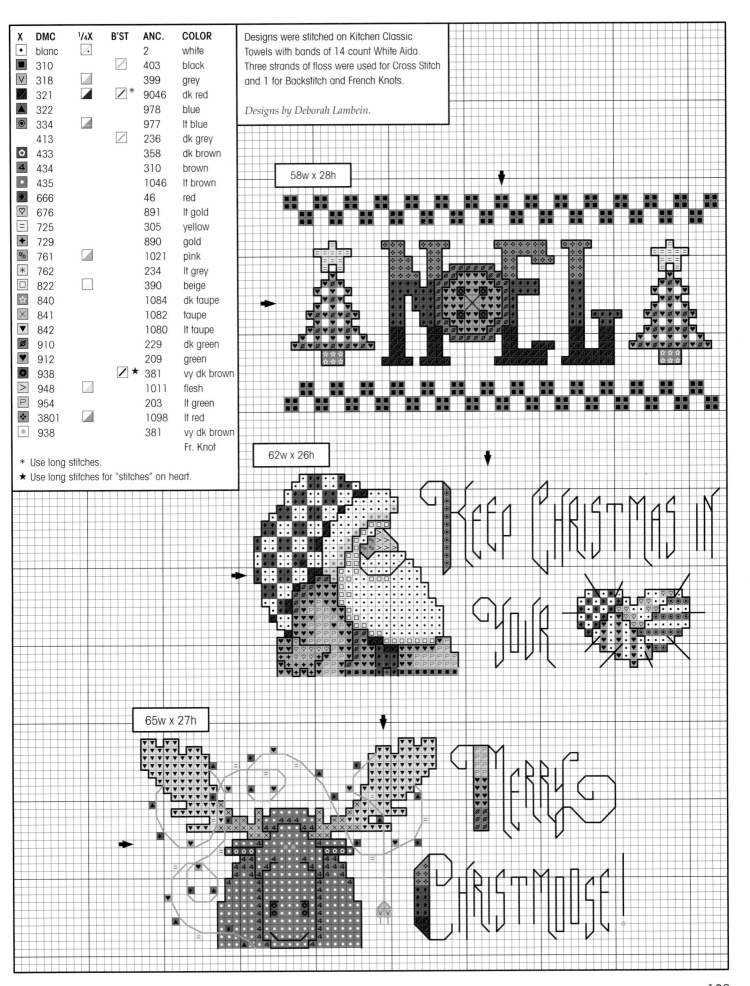

X	DMC	¼X	B'ST	ANC.	COLOR
•	blanc			2	white
■	310			403	black
V	318			399	grey
	321		*	9046	dk red
▲	322			978	blue
◉	334			977	lt blue
	413			236	dk grey
◎	433			358	dk brown
4	434			310	brown
▪	435			1046	lt brown
◆	666			46	red
♡	676			891	lt gold
=	725			305	yellow
✦	729			890	gold
%	761			1021	pink
*	762			234	lt grey
□	822			390	beige
☆	840			1084	dk taupe
✕	841			1082	taupe
▼	842			1080	lt taupe
∅	910			229	dk green
♥	912			209	green
◉	938			381	vy dk brown
>	948			1011	flesh
P	954			203	lt green
❖	3801			1098	lt red
•	938			381	vy dk brown
					Fr. Knot

* Use long stitches.

★ Use long stitches for "stitches" on heart.

Designs were stitched on Kitchen Classic Towels with bands of 14 count White Aida. Three strands of floss were used for Cross Stitch and 1 for Backstitch and French Knots.

Designs by Deborah Lambein.

58w x 28h

62w x 26h

65w x 27h

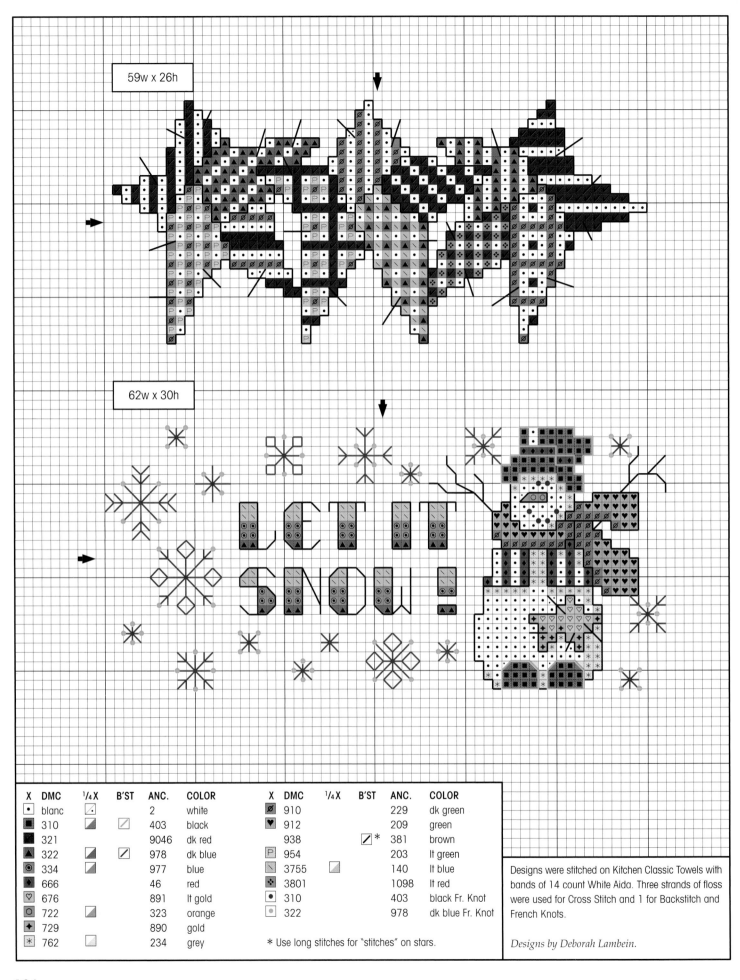

X	DMC	¼X	B'ST	ANC.	COLOR
•	blanc			2	white
■	310			403	black
■	321			9046	dk red
▲	322			978	dk blue
◉	334			977	blue
◆	666			46	red
♥	676			891	lt gold
○	722			323	orange
◆	729			890	gold
✳	762			234	grey

X	DMC	¼X	B'ST	ANC.	COLOR
ø	910			229	dk green
♥	912			209	green
	938		✱	381	brown
P	954			203	lt green
▨	3755			140	lt blue
✤	3801			1098	lt red
•	310			403	black Fr. Knot
◉	322			978	dk blue Fr. Knot

* Use long stitches for "stitches" on stars.

Designs were stitched on Kitchen Classic Towels with bands of 14 count White Aida. Three strands of floss were used for Cross Stitch and 1 for Backstitch and French Knots.

Designs by Deborah Lambein.

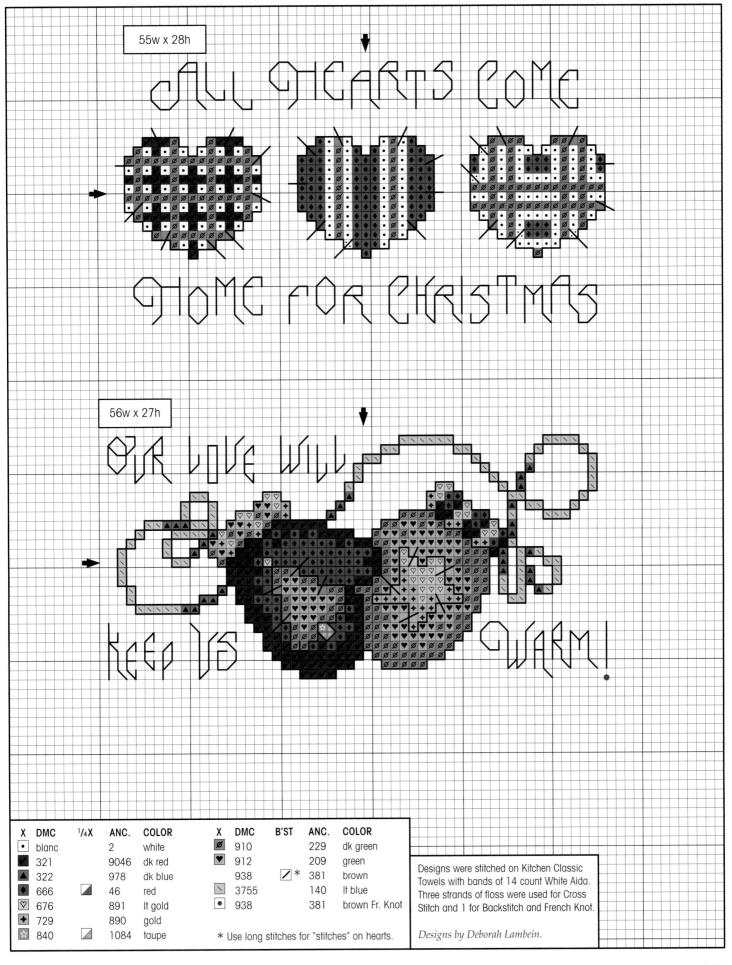

55w x 28h

ALL HEARTS COME

HOME FOR CHRISTMAS

56w x 27h

OUR LOVE WILL

KEEP US WARM!

X	DMC	¼X	ANC.	COLOR	X	DMC	B'ST	ANC.	COLOR
•	blanc		2	white	∅	910		229	dk green
◪	321		9046	dk red	♥	912		209	green
▲	322		978	dk blue		938	◪ *	381	brown
◆	666	◪	46	red	◹	3755		140	lt blue
♡	676		891	lt gold	•	938		381	brown Fr. Knot
◆	729		890	gold					
☆	840	◪	1084	taupe	* Use long stitches for "stitches" on hearts.				

Designs were stitched on Kitchen Classic Towels with bands of 14 count White Aida. Three strands of floss were used for Cross Stitch and 1 for Backstitch and French Knot.

Designs by Deborah Lambein.

Holly
Hand
Towel

Adorned with a "Merry Christmas" message and sprigs of holly, this fingertip towel has traditional Christmas charm. We chose a bold, check towel to accentuate its woodsy colors.

120w x 37h

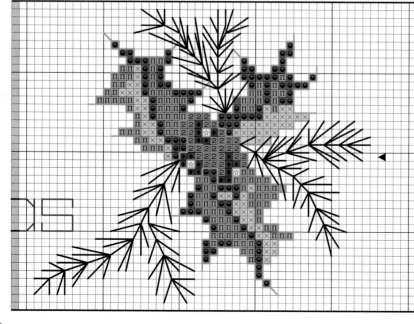

X	DMC	B'ST	ANC.	COLOR
☆	blanc		2	white
2	304		1006	lt red
◆	498	╱*	1005	red
◖	500	╱	683	dk green
	501	╱†	878	green
Π	502		877	lt green
	3371	╱	382	dk brown
✕	3817		875	vy lt green
	Grey area indicates last row of previous section of design.			

*Use **2** strands of floss.

†Work in long stitches.

Design was stitched on a Kitchen Classic Check Towel with a band of 14 count Ivory Aida. Three strands of floss were used for Cross Stitch and 1 for Backstitch except where noted in key.

Design by Krystal Achenbach.

106

Happy Holidays

Make the season merry and bright by embellishing a hand towel with this traditional greeting. The beautiful sentiment is sure to bring a smile to Christmas guests.

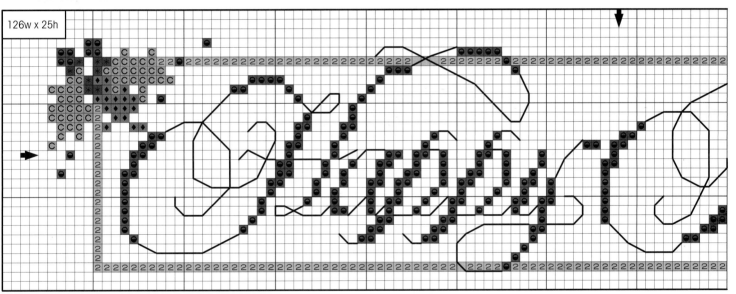

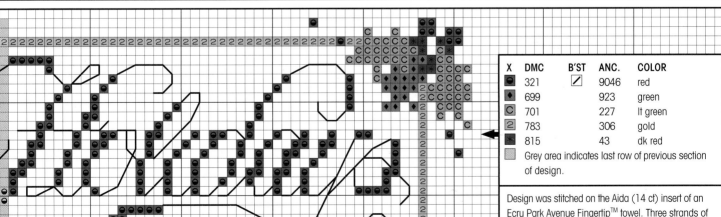

X	DMC	B'ST	ANC.	COLOR
●	321	/	9046	red
◆	699		923	green
C	701		227	lt green
2	783		306	gold
✳	815		43	dk red
	Grey area indicates last row of previous section of design.			

Design was stitched on the Aida (14 ct) insert of an Ecru Park Avenue Fingertip™ towel. Three strands of floss were used for Cross Stitch and 1 for Backstitch.

Design by Sam Hawkins.

Yuletide Greetings

Yuletide messages like these offer a warm way to greet your holiday guests. We used the designs to dress up towels for the bath, but you can also use them on bread covers or table linens.

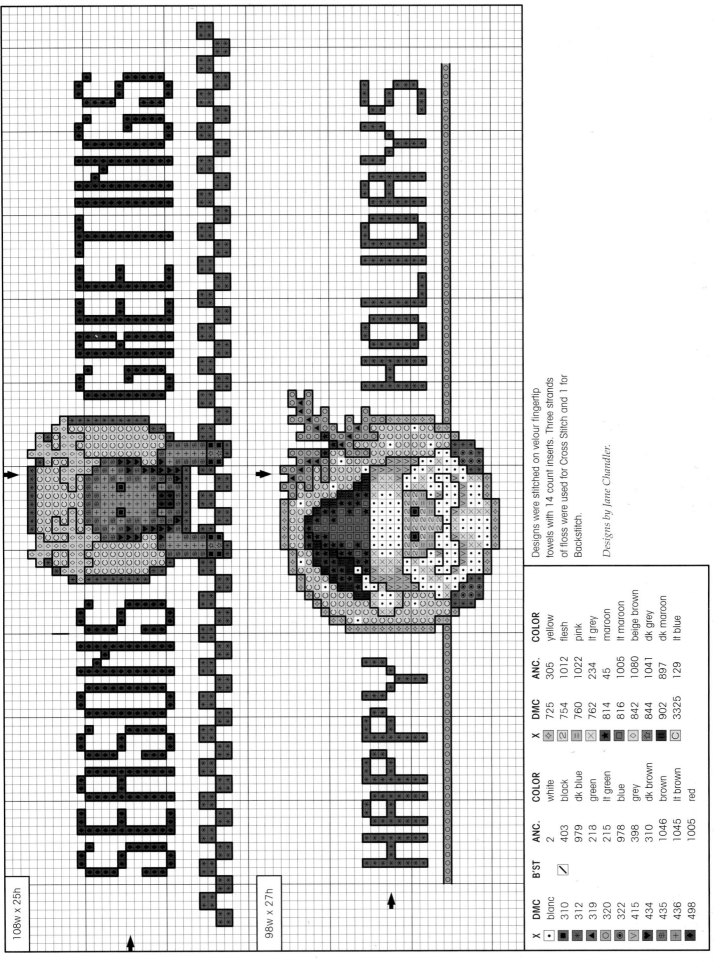

108w x 25h

98w x 27h

Designs were stitched on velour fingertip towels with 14 count inserts. Three strands of floss were used for Cross Stitch and 1 for Backstitch.

Designs by Jane Chandler.

X	DMC	ANC.	COLOR
·	blanc	2	white
■	310	403	black
✳	312	979	dk blue
◀	319	218	green
◐	320	215	lt green
◉	322	978	blue
▷	415	398	grey
▶	434	310	dk brown
$	435	1046	brown
+	436	1045	lt brown
◆	498	1005	red

X	DMC	ANC.	COLOR
◇	725	305	yellow
2	754	1012	flesh
=	760	1022	pink
×	762	234	lt grey
★	814	45	maroon
□	816	1005	lt maroon
◇	842	1080	beige brown
✿	844	1041	dk grey
▓	902	897	dk maroon
C	3325	129	lt blue

B'ST		
╱		

Little Lambs

Stitched on a bread cloth, these sweet little lambs remind us of the scripture in which Jesus instructs us to "feed my lambs," meaning His children. What a fitting way to break bread with loved ones during the holiday.

X	DMC	B'ST	ANC.	COLOR
☆	blanc		2	white
■	310	✓	403	black
★	311		148	blue
◉	321		9046	red
◣	367		217	green
=	822		390	cream
✳	844		1041	grey

Grey area indicates beginning of fringe.

Design was stitched on a Rich Cranberry Solid Royal Classic Bread Cover (14 ct). Three strands of floss were used for Cross Stitch and 1 for Backstitch. Design was stitched 3/4" from outer edge of fringe; borders were extended along edges of bread covers.

Design by Jane Chandler.

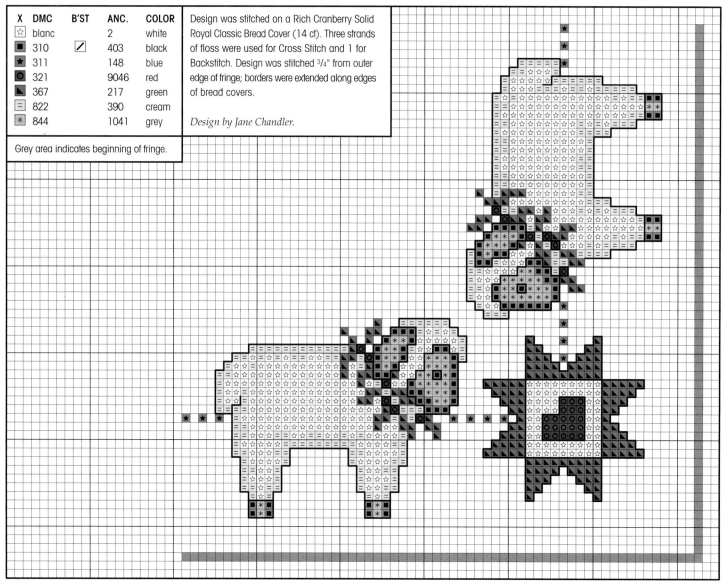

Snowy Day Surprise

While you may never satisfy the desire to preserve a sparkling snowflake, you can bring a few of these winter beauties into your kitchen with our simplistic mug and towel set. Captured in their splendor, these crystals won't melt — even when encircling a mug of steamy cider or hanging in a warm, cozy kitchen.

X	DMC	B'ST	ANC.	COLOR
★	322	✎	978	blue
✳	3325		129	lt blue

Note: For all projects, 2 strands of floss were used for Cross Stitch and Backstitch.

Towel: The design was stitched on the 14 ct insert of a White Fingertip™ towel.

Mug: The design was stitched on a 10¼" x 3½" White Vinyl-Weave™ (14 ct) mug insert. It was inserted in a White Stitch-A-Mug. Remove stitched piece before washing mug.

Design by Deborah Lambein.

65w x 30h

111

For the Christmas Kitchen

Baking is synonymous with Christmas, so why not stitch up a batch of potholders to help you with your holiday cooking. These four designs are sure to season your holiday with flavor!

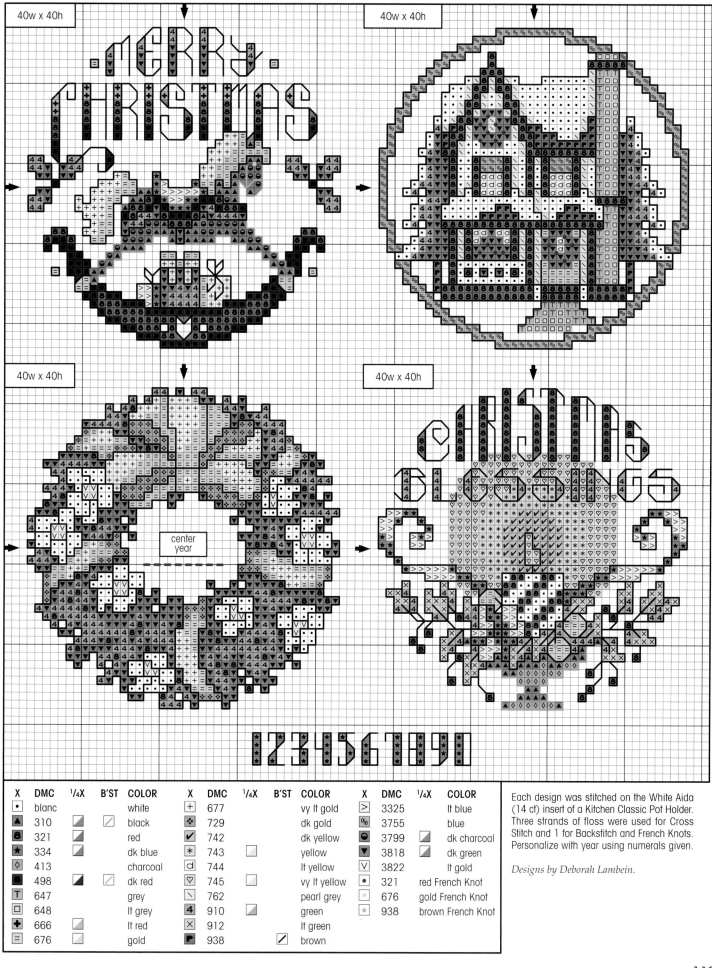

X	DMC	¼X	B'ST	COLOR	X	DMC	¼X	B'ST	COLOR	X	DMC	¼X	COLOR
•	blanc			white	+	677			vy lt gold	>	3325		lt blue
▲	310	◢	/	black	❖	729			dk gold	%	3755		blue
8	321	◢		red	✔	742			dk yellow	⊖	3799	◢	dk charcoal
★	334	◢		dk blue	*	743			yellow	▼	3818	◢	dk green
◇	413			charcoal	d	744			lt yellow	V	3822		lt gold
■	498	◢	/	dk red	♡	745			vy lt yellow	•	321		red French Knot
T	647			grey	\	762			pearl grey	⊡	676		gold French Knot
☐	648			lt grey	4	910			green	⊡	938		brown French Knot
+	666			lt red	✕	912			lt green				
=	676			gold	◪	938			brown				
≡	676	◢	/	gold	/				brown				

Each design was stitched on the White Aida (14 ct) insert of a Kitchen Classic Pot Holder. Three strands of floss were used for Cross Stitch and 1 for Backstitch and French Knots. Personalize with year using numerals given.

Designs by Deborah Lambein.

Homespun
Warmth

Your holiday goodies will stay toasty from the oven to the table wrapped in one of these homespun bread cloths. And their North Woods charm will tempt you to display them year-round.

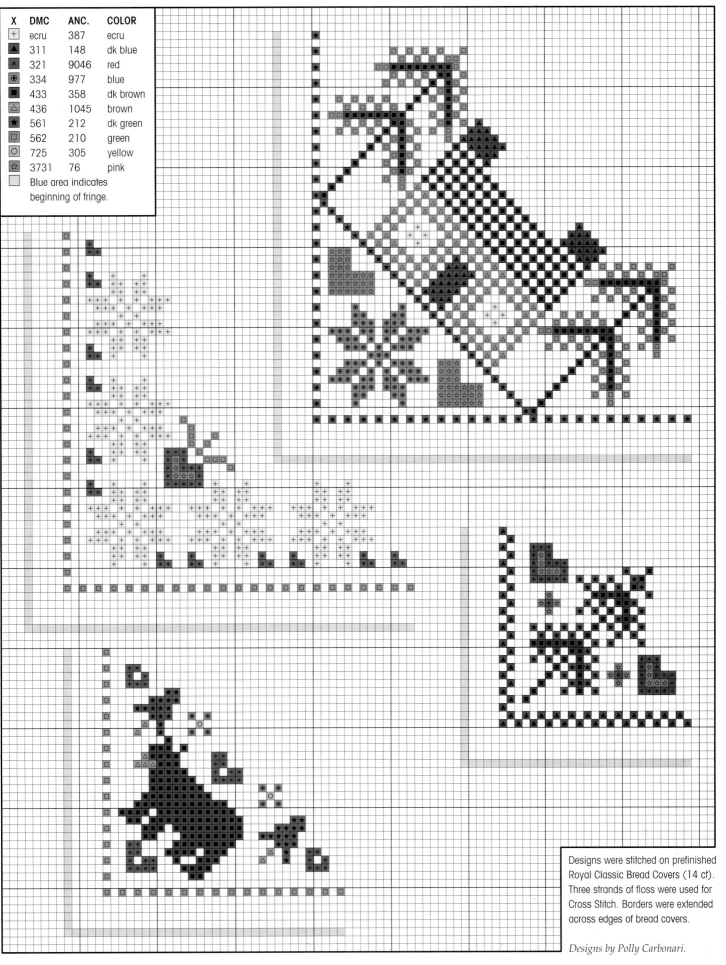

X	DMC	ANC.	COLOR
+	ecru	387	ecru
▲	311	148	dk blue
✳	321	9046	red
⊙	334	977	blue
■	433	358	dk brown
△	436	1045	brown
★	561	212	dk green
▢	562	210	green
○	725	305	yellow
☆	3731	76	pink

Blue area indicates beginning of fringe.

Designs were stitched on prefinished Royal Classic Bread Covers (14 ct). Three strands of floss were used for Cross Stitch. Borders were extended across edges of bread covers.

Designs by Polly Carbonari.

A Heartfelt Gift

Accompanied by a Nativity scene, this spiritual poem makes a fitting addition to your Christmas celebration. It brings the true reason for the season to the observance.

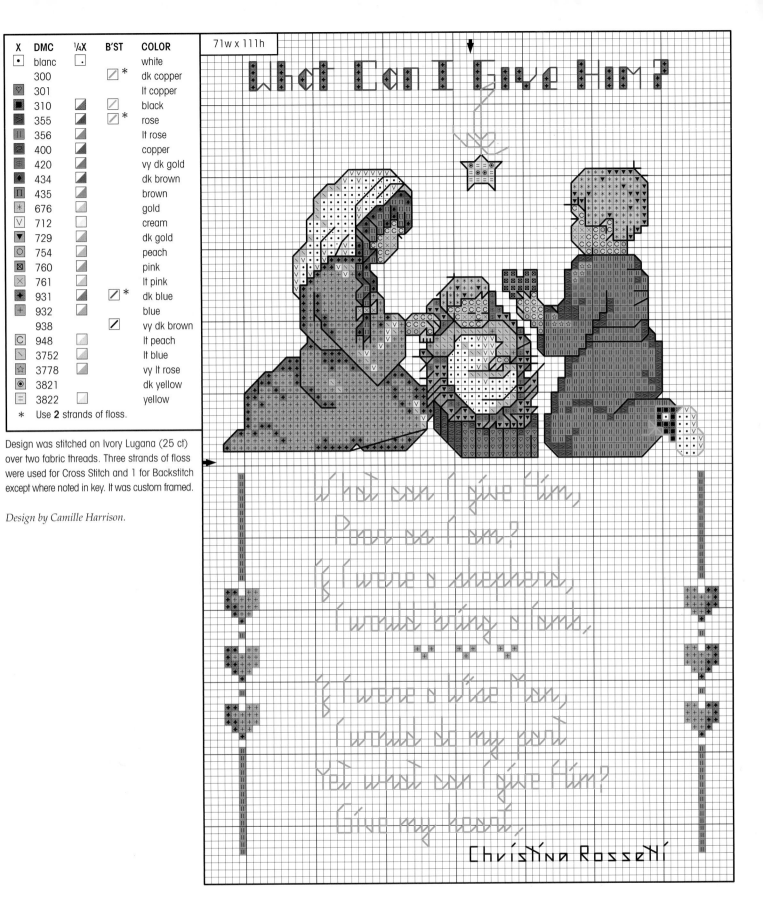

X	DMC	¼X	B'ST	COLOR
•	blanc	•		white
	300		⊘ *	dk copper
♡	301			lt copper
■	310	◪	⊘ *	black
▶	355	◪	⊘ *	rose
‖	356	◪		lt rose
2	400	◪		copper
$	420	◪		vy dk gold
◆	434	◪		dk brown
∏	435	◪		brown
✳	676	◪		gold
V	712	◪		cream
▼	729	◪		dk gold
○	754	◪		peach
⊠	760	◪		pink
✕	761	◪		lt pink
✦	931	◪	⊘ *	dk blue
✛	932	◪		blue
	938		⊘	vy dk brown
C	948	◪		lt peach
⋮	3752	◪		lt blue
☆	3778	◪		vy lt rose
⊙	3821	◪		dk yellow
⊟	3822	◪		yellow

* Use **2** strands of floss.

Design was stitched on Ivory Lugana (25 ct) over two fabric threads. Three strands of floss were used for Cross Stitch and 1 for Backstitch except where noted in key. It was custom framed.

Design by Camille Harrison.

71w x 111h

What Can I Give Him?

What can I give Him,
Poor as I am?
If I were a shepherd,
I would bring a lamb,

If I were a Wise Man,
I would do my part
Yet what can I give Him?
Give my heart.

Christina Rossetti

Delightful Gifts

Much of the joy of Christmas is in giving — giving your heart in a handmade gift that simply says, "I'm thinking of you and wishing you a happy holiday." This collection of gift ideas includes dozens of designs that will help you convey those sentiments to family and friends. You'll find special ideas for trimming your presents, too.

to: Nick
from: Mom

Please come home for Christmas!

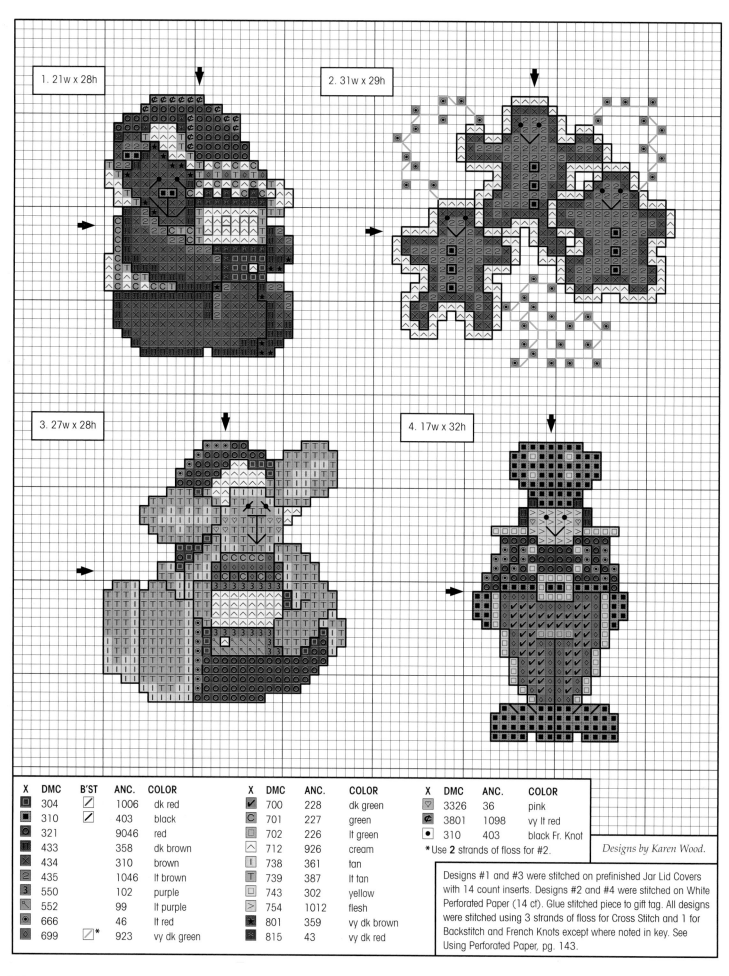

1. 21w x 28h

2. 31w x 29h

3. 27w x 28h

4. 17w x 32h

X	DMC	B'ST	ANC.	COLOR		X	DMC	ANC.	COLOR		X	DMC	ANC.	COLOR
▣	304	⟋	1006	dk red		✔	700	228	dk green		♡	3326	36	pink
■	310	⟋	403	black		C	701	227	green		¢	3801	1098	vy lt red
⊙	321		9046	red		▢	702	226	lt green		●	310	403	black Fr. Knot
▥	433		358	dk brown		∧	712	926	cream					
✕	434		310	brown		I	738	361	tan		*Use 2 strands of floss for #2.			
2	435		1046	lt brown		T	739	387	lt tan					
3	550		102	purple		▢	743	302	yellow		*Designs by Karen Wood.*			
◣	552		99	lt purple		>	754	1012	flesh					
⊙	666		46	lt red		★	801	359	vy dk brown					
◆	699	⟋*	923	vy dk green		✳	815	43	vy dk red					

Designs #1 and #3 were stitched on prefinished Jar Lid Covers with 14 count inserts. Designs #2 and #4 were stitched on White Perforated Paper (14 cf). Glue stitched piece to gift tag. All designs were stitched using 3 strands of floss for Cross Stitch and 1 for Backstitch and French Knots except where noted in key. See Using Perforated Paper, pg. 143.

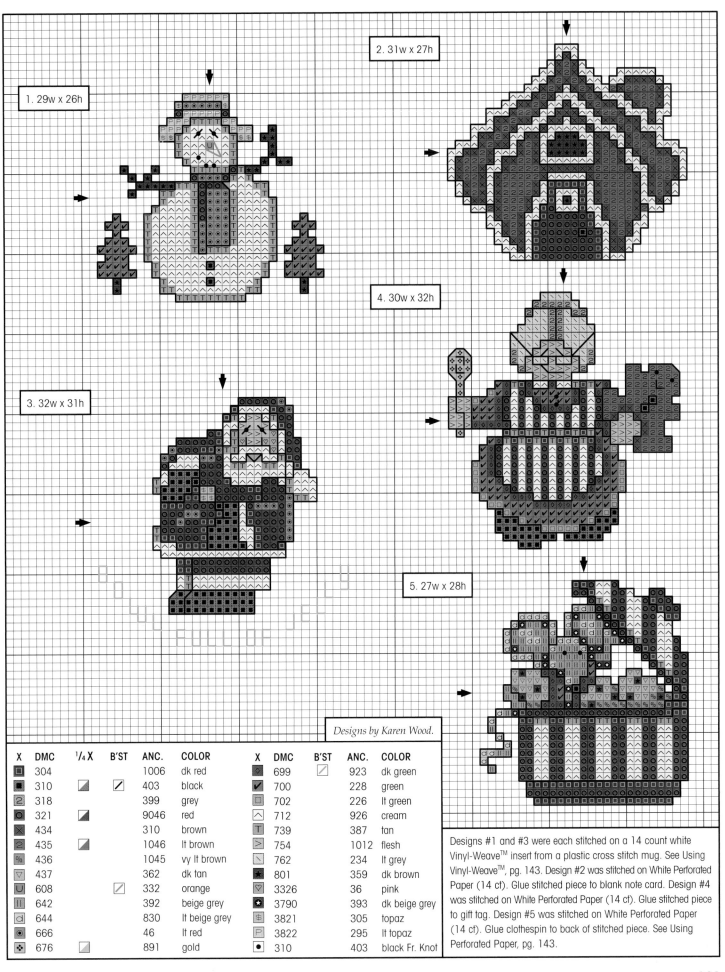

1. 29w x 26h

2. 31w x 27h

3. 32w x 31h

4. 30w x 32h

5. 27w x 28h

Designs by Karen Wood.

X	DMC	¼ X	B'ST	ANC.	COLOR	X	DMC	B'ST	ANC.	COLOR
▣	304			1006	dk red	◆	699	◿	923	dk green
■	310	◿	◿	403	black	✔	700		228	green
2	318			399	grey	▣	702		226	lt green
◎	321	◿		9046	red	∧	712		926	cream
✕	434			310	brown	T	739		387	tan
2	435	◿		1046	lt brown	▷	754		1012	flesh
%	436			1045	vy lt brown	◸	762		234	lt grey
▽	437			362	dk tan	★	801		359	dk brown
U	608		◿	332	orange	♡	3326		36	pink
‖	642			392	beige grey	✺	3790		393	dk beige grey
d	644			830	lt beige grey	$	3821		305	topaz
◉	666			46	lt red	P	3822		295	lt topaz
✤	676	◿		891	gold	●	310		403	black Fr. Knot

Designs #1 and #3 were each stitched on a 14 count white Vinyl-Weave™ insert from a plastic cross stitch mug. See Using Vinyl-Weave™, pg. 143. Design #2 was stitched on White Perforated Paper (14 ct). Glue stitched piece to blank note card. Design #4 was stitched on White Perforated Paper (14 ct). Glue stitched piece to gift tag. Design #5 was stitched on White Perforated Paper (14 ct). Glue clothespin to back of stitched piece. See Using Perforated Paper, pg. 143.

North Pole Pals

Lend a merry touch to a friend's holiday collection with our festive mug! As their faces radiate a warm Christmas glow, this cute Santa and his trusty reindeer will surely bring glad tidings of good cheer.

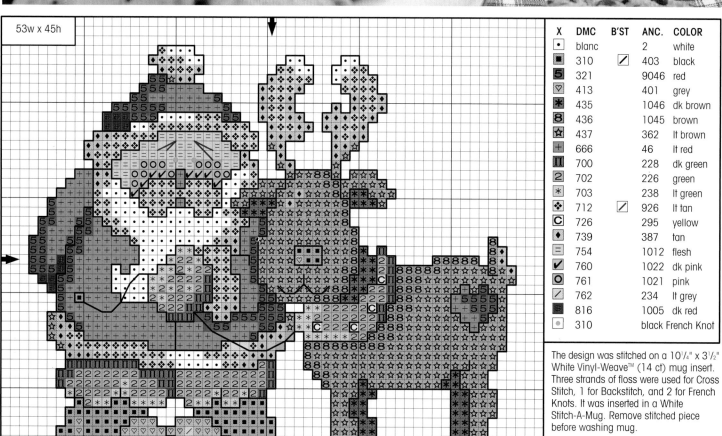

53w x 45h

X	DMC	B'ST	ANC.	COLOR
•	blanc		2	white
■	310	╱	403	black
5	321		9046	red
♡	413		401	grey
✳	435		1046	dk brown
8	436		1045	brown
☆	437		362	lt brown
+	666		46	lt red
Ⅱ	700		228	dk green
2	702		226	green
✱	703		238	lt green
◆	712	╱	926	lt tan
C	726		295	yellow
◆	739		387	tan
=	754		1012	flesh
✔	760		1022	dk pink
O	761		1021	pink
╱	762		234	lt grey
▦	816		1005	dk red
◉	310			black French Knot

The design was stitched on a 10¼" x 3½" White Vinyl-Weave™ (14 ct) mug insert. Three strands of floss were used for Cross Stitch, 1 for Backstitch, and 2 for French Knots. It was inserted in a White Stitch-A-Mug. Remove stitched piece before washing mug.

Design by Kathy Rueger.

Li'l Santa Stick-ups

Give two gifts in one by topping off gaily wrapped presents with our cute little Santa magnets. Featuring portraits of jolly old St. Nick, the quick-to-stitch accents bring to mind a "Ho-Ho-Ho" and serve as thoughtful holiday keepsakes.

X	DMC	B'ST	ANC.	COLOR
•	blanc		2	white
★	223		895	dk pink
▲	224		893	pink
◥	304		1006	red
■	310	╱	403	black
◒	367		217	green
✳	415		398	grey
E	815		43	dk red
+	928		274	lt blue
C	948		1011	peach
⊙	304			red French Knot

Note: Both projects were stitched using 3 strands of floss for Cross Stitch and 1 for Backstitch and French Knots. They were made into magnets.
Design #1 was stitched on a 3" x 5" piece of White Vinyl-Weave™ (14 ct).
Design #2 was stitched on a 3½" square of White Vinyl-Weave™ (14 ct).
To assemble magnet, center stitched piece on adhesive magnet and press in place. Trim one square from edge of design.

Designs by Penny Duff.

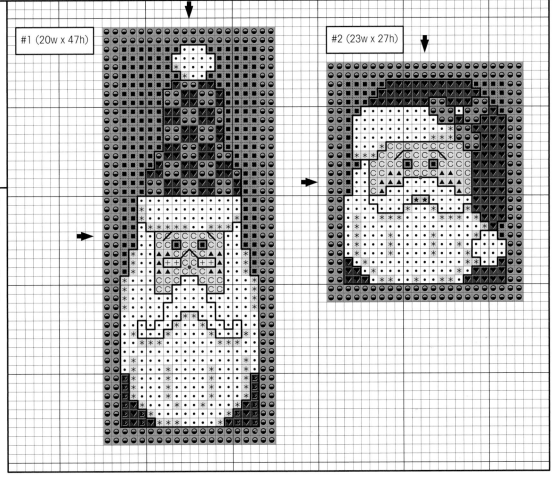

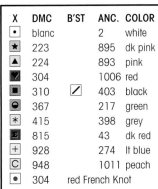

Cheery Cups

You'll serve up the perfect present when you deliver one of these holiday mugs laden with treats or the makings for a favorite drink. The cheery cups also make great pencil holders for the office.

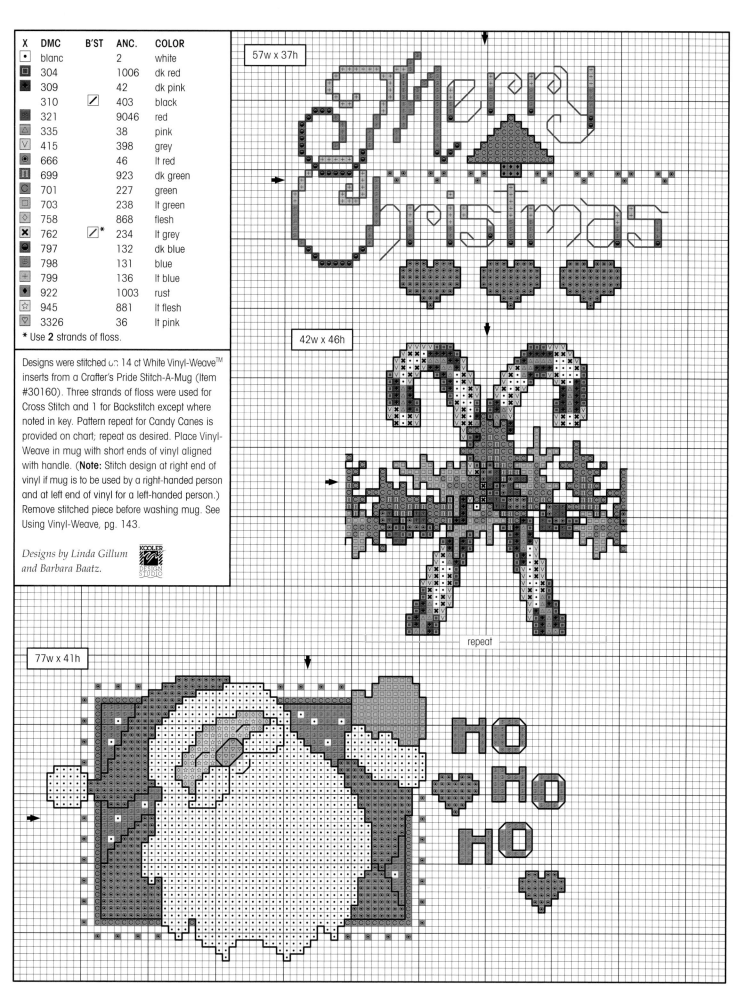

X	DMC	B'ST	ANC.	COLOR
•	blanc		2	white
◻	304		1006	dk red
◆	309		42	dk pink
	310	✎	403	black
✳	321		9046	red
△	335		38	pink
V	415		398	grey
◉	666		46	lt red
Π	699		923	dk green
C	701		227	green
▢	703		238	lt green
◇	758		868	flesh
✕	762	✎*	234	lt grey
◐	797		132	dk blue
⑤	798		131	blue
+	799		136	lt blue
◆	922		1003	rust
☆	945		881	lt flesh
♡	3326		36	lt pink

* Use 2 strands of floss.

Designs were stitched on 14 ct White Vinyl-Weave™ inserts from a Crafter's Pride Stitch-A-Mug (Item #30160). Three strands of floss were used for Cross Stitch and 1 for Backstitch except where noted in key. Pattern repeat for Candy Canes is provided on chart; repeat as desired. Place Vinyl-Weave in mug with short ends of vinyl aligned with handle. (**Note:** Stitch design at right end of vinyl if mug is to be used by a right-handed person and at left end of vinyl for a left-handed person.) Remove stitched piece before washing mug. See Using Vinyl-Weave, pg. 143.

Designs by Linda Gillum and Barbara Baatz.

KOOLER DESIGN STUDIO

57w x 37h

42w x 46h

repeat

77w x 41h

for the Hostess

A friend's kitchen will be filled with holiday magic when this Christmas gift set is received. Three jar toppers, a fingertip towel, and a framed piece make up the joyful assortment.

X	DMC	¹/₄X	B'ST	ANC.	COLOR	X	DMC	¹/₄X	B'ST	ANC.	COLOR	X	DMC	¹/₄X	B'ST	ANC.	COLOR
	blanc			2	white		640			903	dk beige		783			306	dk gold
	ecru			387	ecru		642			392	beige		814			45	vy dk red
	310			403	black		644			830	lt beige		815			43	dk red
	311			148	blue		676			891	gold		822			390	vy lt beige
	319			218	green		725			305	yellow		930			1035	grey blue
	321			9046	lt red		754			1012	flesh		931			1034	lt grey blue
	349			13	coral		758			868	lt flesh		943			188	aqua
	367			217	lt green		760			1022	pink		991			1076	dk aqua
	402			1047	rust		761			1021	lt pink		992			1072	lt aqua
	498			1005	red		762			234	grey		993			1070	vy lt aqua

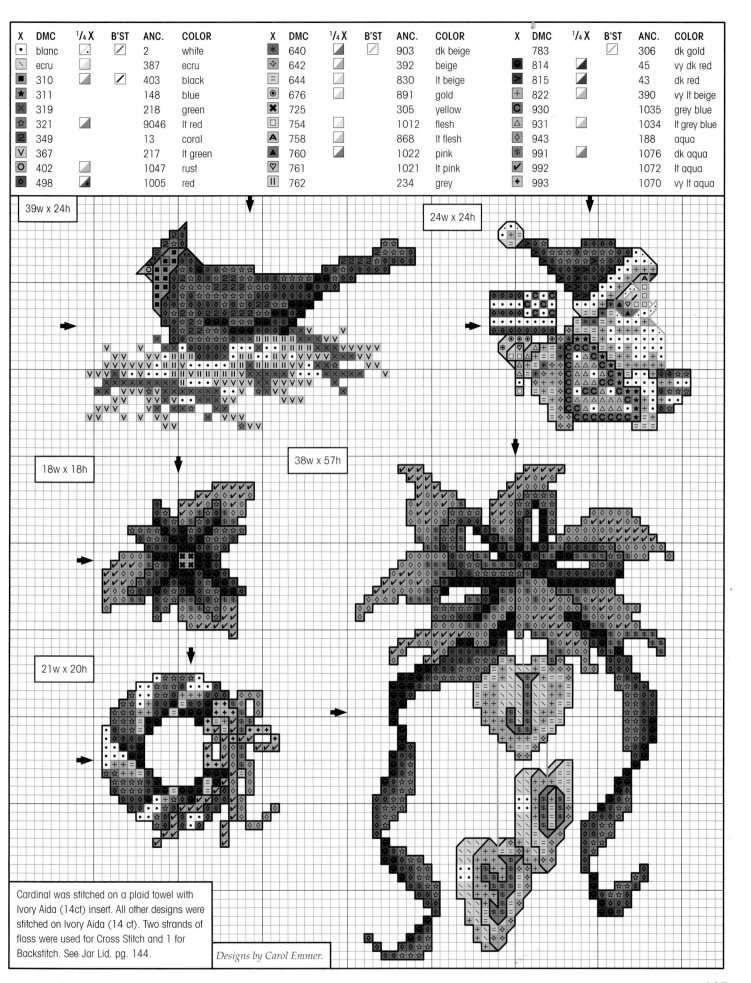

39w x 24h

24w x 24h

18w x 18h

38w x 57h

21w x 20h

Cardinal was stitched on a plaid towel with Ivory Aida (14ct) insert. All other designs were stitched on Ivory Aida (14 ct). Two strands of floss were used for Cross Stitch and 1 for Backstitch. See Jar Lid, pg. 144.

Designs by Carol Emmer.

Poinsettia *Pizzazz*

With its regal red coloring and splendid blooms, the poinsettia embodies the essence of Yuletide tradition.
Our festive gift bag, bread cloth, and jar lid capture the classic beauty of this vibrant Christmas flower.

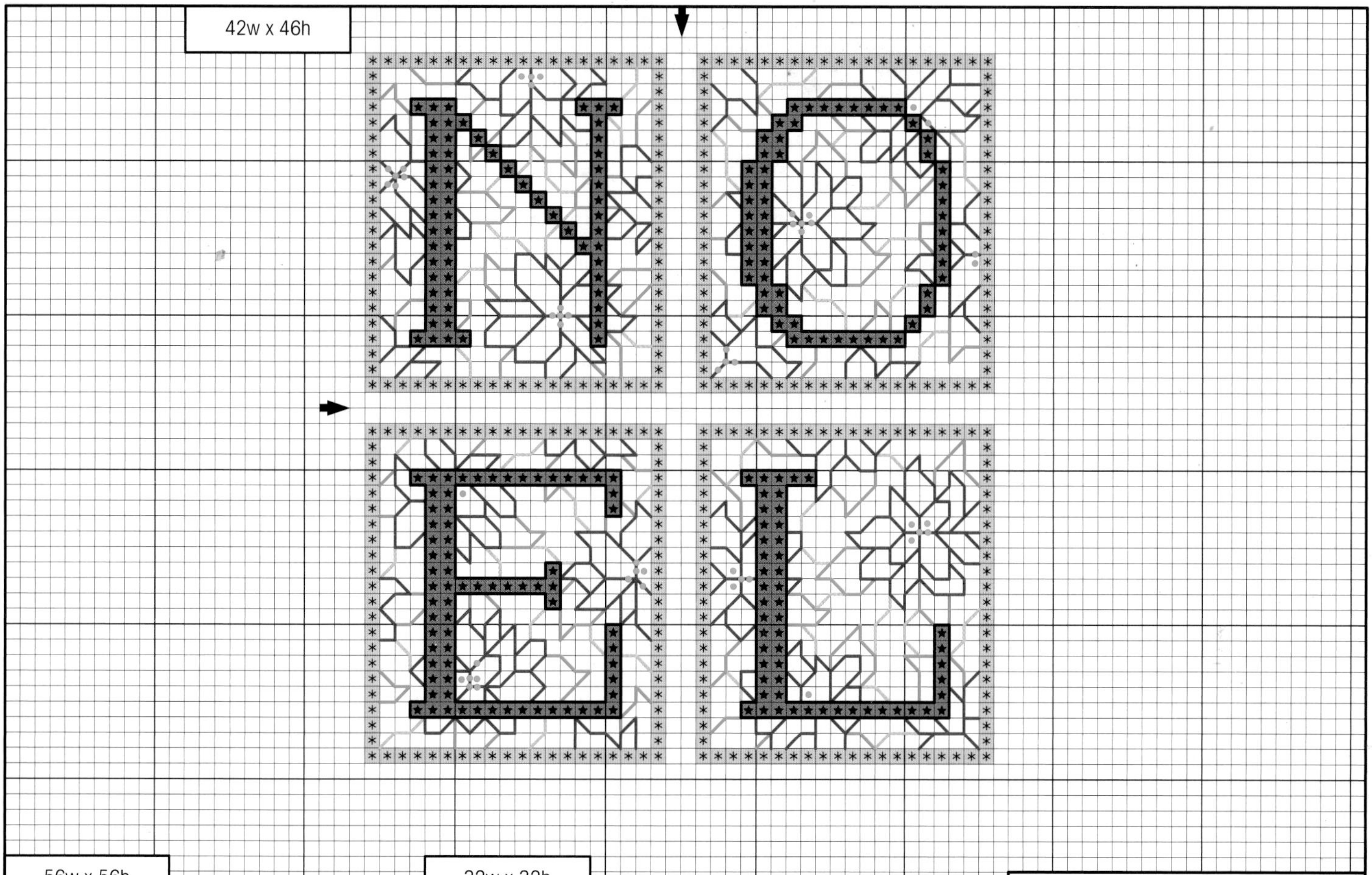

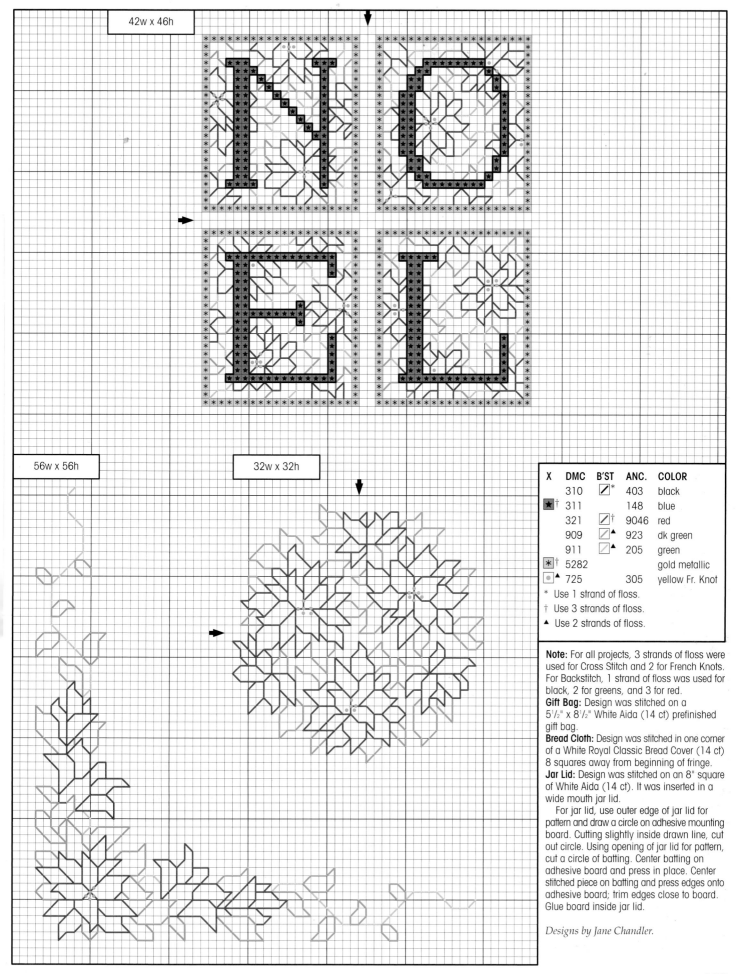

42w x 46h

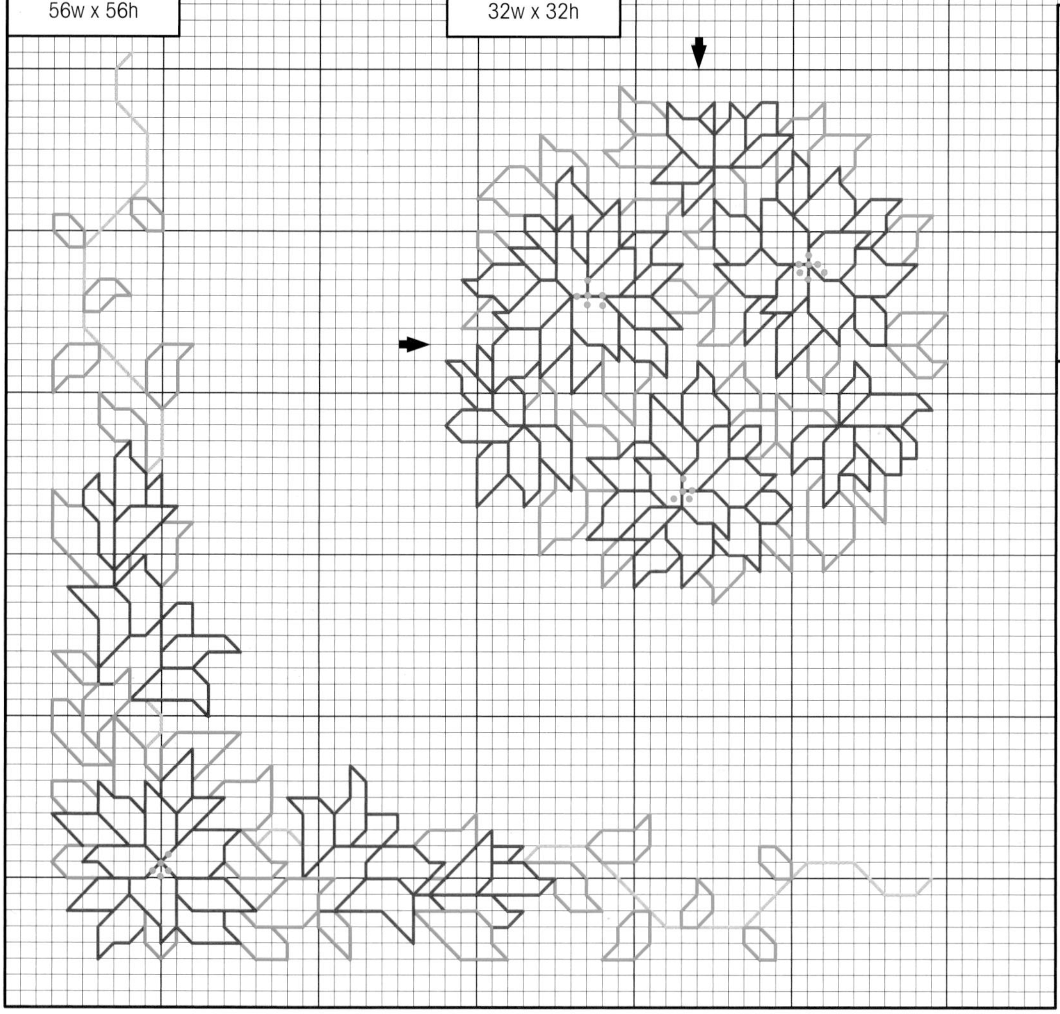

56w x 56h
32w x 32h

X	DMC	B'ST	ANC.	COLOR
	310	[line]*	403	black
[star symbol]†	311		148	blue
	321	[line]†	9046	red
	909	[line]▲	923	dk green
	911	[line]▲	205	green
[asterisk symbol]†	5282			gold metallic
[dot symbol]▲	725		305	yellow Fr. Knot

* Use 1 strand of floss.
† Use 3 strands of floss.
▲ Use 2 strands of floss.

Note: For all projects, 3 strands of floss were used for Cross Stitch and 2 for French Knots. For Backstitch, 1 strand of floss was used for black, 2 for greens, and 3 for red.

Gift Bag: Design was stitched on a 5½" x 8½" White Aida (14 ct) prefinished gift bag.

Bread Cloth: Design was stitched in one corner of a White Royal Classic Bread Cover (14 ct) 8 squares away from beginning of fringe.

Jar Lid: Design was stitched on an 8" square of White Aida (14 ct). It was inserted in a wide mouth jar lid.

For jar lid, use outer edge of jar lid for pattern and draw a circle on adhesive mounting board. Cutting slightly inside drawn line, cut out circle. Using opening of jar lid for pattern, cut a circle of batting. Center batting on adhesive board and press in place. Center stitched piece on batting and press edges onto adhesive board; trim edges close to board. Glue board inside jar lid.

Designs by Jane Chandler.

Heartwarming Snowman

This friendly snowman has a big heart for sharing! Sit him atop a jar of Christmas treats for a gift that's twice as sweet.

X	DMC	1/4X	B'ST	ANC.	COLOR
•	blanc	·		2	white
▲	224			893	pink
▼	304			1006	red
■	310		╱	403	black
⊖	319			218	dk green
▢	367			217	green
%	415			398	lt grey
2	921	◪		1003	orange
★	932			1033	blue

The design was stitched on a 6" square of Antique White Aida (14 ct). Three strands of floss were used for Cross Stitch and 1 for Backstitch. It was inserted in a wide mouth jar lid.

For jar lid, use outer edge of jar lid for pattern and draw a circle on adhesive mounting board. Cutting slightly inside drawn line, cut out circle. Using opening of jar lid for pattern, cut a circle of batting. Center batting on adhesive board and press in place. Center stitched piece on batting and press edges onto adhesive board; trim edges close to board. Glue board inside jar lid.

Design by Penny Duff.

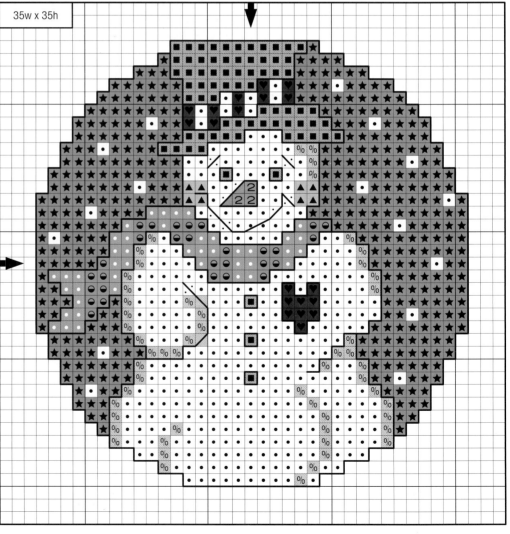

35w x 35h

Holly-Jolly Traditions

Display delectable fares or pretty presents in jars topped with one of our holly-jolly jar lids. Finished with designs that feature traditional Christmas greenery, the cheery trio will add an extra holiday "twist" to your tokens!

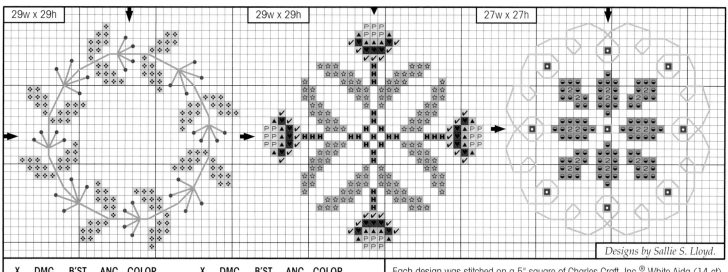

Designs by Sallie S. Lloyd.

X	DMC	B'ST	ANC.	COLOR	X	DMC	B'ST	ANC.	COLOR
◆	304	◢	1006	dk red	❖	368		214	lt green
◐	319		218	vy dk green	H	500		683	dk blue green
2	320		215	green	☆	502		877	blue green
▼	321		9046	red	✔	503		876	lt blue green
▲	350		11	dk peach		5282	◢		metallic gold
P	352		9	peach	●	321			red French knot
	367	◢*	217	dk green					* Use 2 strands of floss.

Each design was stitched on a 5" square of Charles Craft, Inc.® White Aida (14 ct). Two strands of floss were used for Cross Stitch, 1 for Backstitch, and 4 for French Knots, unless otherwise noted in the color key. They were inserted in small mouth jar lids.

For jar lid, use outer edge of jar lid for pattern and draw a circle on adhesive mounting board. Cutting slightly inside drawn line, cut out circle. Using opening of jar lid for pattern, cut a circle of batting. Center batting on adhesive board and press in place. Center stitched piece on batting and press edges onto adhesive board; trim edges close to board. Glue board inside jar lid.

Goodies for Santa

St. Nick will be inclined to leave bunches of Yuletide treasures when he finds these sweet surprises. Delightfully displayed in a cheery ensemble, your tasty morsels are just the thing to send Santa and his reindeer merrily on their way!

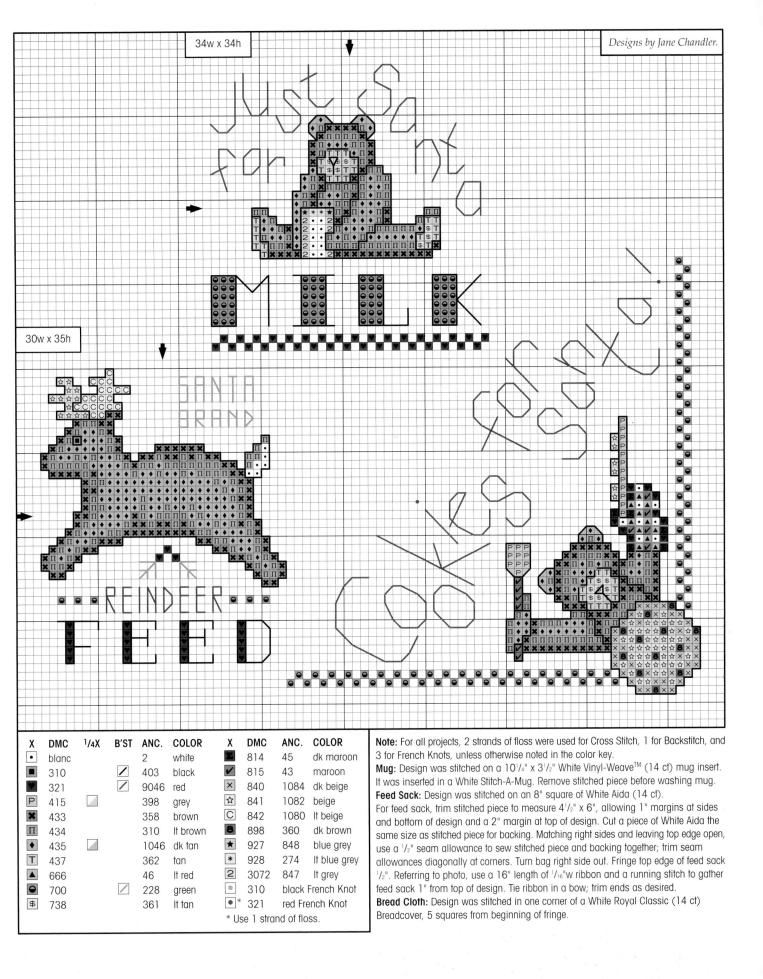

X	DMC	1/4X	B'ST	ANC.	COLOR	X	DMC	ANC.	COLOR
•	blanc			2	white	■	814	45	dk maroon
■	310		✓	403	black	✓	815	43	maroon
▼	321		✓	9046	red	✗	840	1084	dk beige
P	415	◿		398	grey	☆	841	1082	beige
✗	433			358	brown	C	842	1080	lt beige
⊓	434			310	lt brown	8	898	360	dk brown
◆	435	◿		1046	dk tan	★	927	848	blue grey
T	437			362	tan	＊	928	274	lt blue grey
▲	666			46	lt red	2	3072	847	lt grey
◉	700		✓	228	green	◉	310		black French Knot
$	738			361	lt tan	◉*	321		red French Knot
							* Use 1 strand of floss.		

Note: For all projects, 2 strands of floss were used for Cross Stitch, 1 for Backstitch, and 3 for French Knots, unless otherwise noted in the color key.

Mug: Design was stitched on a 10¼" x 3½" White Vinyl-Weave™ (14 ct) mug insert. It was inserted in a White Stitch-A-Mug. Remove stitched piece before washing mug.

Feed Sack: Design was stitched on an 8" square of White Aida (14 ct).

For feed sack, trim stitched piece to measure 4½" x 6", allowing 1" margins at sides and bottom of design and a 2" margin at top of design. Cut a piece of White Aida the same size as stitched piece for backing. Matching right sides and leaving top edge open, use a ½" seam allowance to sew stitched piece and backing together; trim seam allowances diagonally at corners. Turn bag right side out. Fringe top edge of feed sack ½". Referring to photo, use a 16" length of 1/16"w ribbon and a running stitch to gather feed sack 1" from top of design. Tie ribbon in a bow; trim ends as desired.

Bread Cloth: Design was stitched in one corner of a White Royal Classic (14 ct) Breadcover, 5 squares from beginning of fringe.

Jiffy Jar Toppers

In a pinch and need a quick gift? These festive jar toppers stitch up in a snap for sweet little tokens of affection. Fill the jar with a favorite candy and your gift is ready!

X	DMC	¼X	B'ST	ANC.	COLOR	X	DMC	¼X	B'ST	ANC.	COLOR
•	blanc	•		2	white	▼	740			316	orange
⊓	209			109	lavender	✕	742			303	dk yellow
✳	211			342	lt lavender	○	744			301	yellow
	413		╱	236	grey	✕	762			234	lt grey
◆	666			46	lt red	⊖	816		╱	1005	red
▲	699		╱	923	dk green	+	3705			35	pink
✦	701			227	green	+	3823			386	lt yellow
◉	704			256	lt green						

Designs were stitched on White Aida (14 ct). Three strands of floss were used for Cross Stitch and 1 for Backstitch. See Jar Lid, pg. 144.

Designs by Linda Gillum and Barbara Baatz.

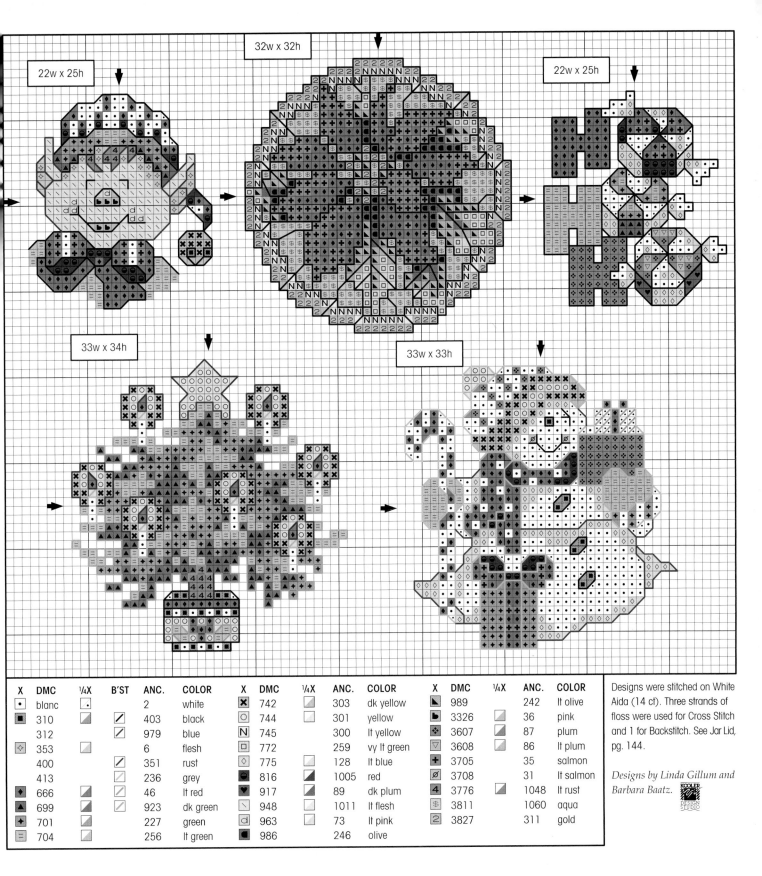

X	DMC	¼X	B'ST	ANC.	COLOR	X	DMC	¼X	ANC.	COLOR	X	DMC	¼X	ANC.	COLOR
•	blanc	•		2	white	✖	742	◪	303	dk yellow	◣	989		242	lt olive
■	310	◪	✎	403	black	○	744	◪	301	yellow	◗	3326	◪	36	pink
	312		✎	979	blue	N	745		300	lt yellow	✦	3607		87	plum
◈	353	◪		6	flesh	▣	772		259	vy lt green	▽	3608	◪	86	lt plum
	400		✎	351	rust	◇	775		128	lt blue	✚	3705		35	salmon
	413		✎	236	grey	◕	816	◪	1005	red	∅	3708		31	lt salmon
◆	666	◪	✎	46	lt red	▼	917		89	dk plum	4	3776	◪	1048	lt rust
▲	699	◪	✎	923	dk green	◣	948		1011	lt flesh	$	3811		1060	aqua
✦	701	◪		227	green	d	963		73	lt pink	2	3827		311	gold
=	704	◪		256	lt green	◑	986		246	olive					

Designs were stitched on White Aida (14 ct). Three strands of floss were used for Cross Stitch and 1 for Backstitch. See Jar Lid, pg. 144.

Designs by Linda Gillum and Barbara Baatz.

A Partridge in a Pear Tree

On the first day of Christmas (or any day!), send freshly baked goodies wrapped in our "partridge in a pear tree" bread cover. As an added bonus, tuck in a jar of yummies topped with a matching jar lid.

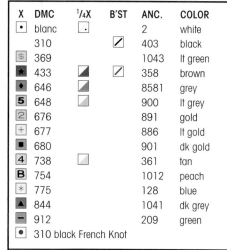

X	DMC	¼X	B'ST	ANC.	COLOR
•	blanc	.		2	white
	310		╱	403	black
$	369			1043	lt green
★	433	◢	╱	358	brown
◆	646	◢		8581	grey
5	648	◢		900	lt grey
2	676			891	gold
+	677			886	lt gold
■	680			901	dk gold
4	738	◢		361	tan
B	754			1012	peach
*	775			128	blue
▲	844			1041	dk grey
–	912			209	green
●	310 black French Knot				

Design was stitched on an Ivory Sal-Em™ Cloth (14 ct) bread cover 4 fabric threads from machine-stitched lines. The partridge was stitched on Ivory Aida (14 ct). It was inserted in a wide mouth jar lid. See Jar Lid, pg. 144. Two strands of floss were used for Cross Stitch and 1 for Backstitch and French Knot.

Design by Carol Emmer.

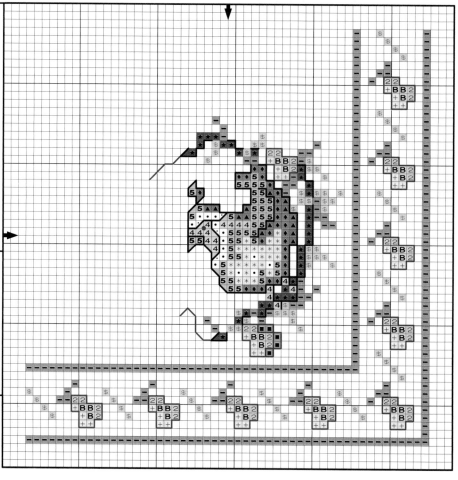

Christmas Alphabet

Personalizing gifts for friends and family is a cinch using our festive alphabets. The letters can also be used to accent accessories with a medley of merry messages.

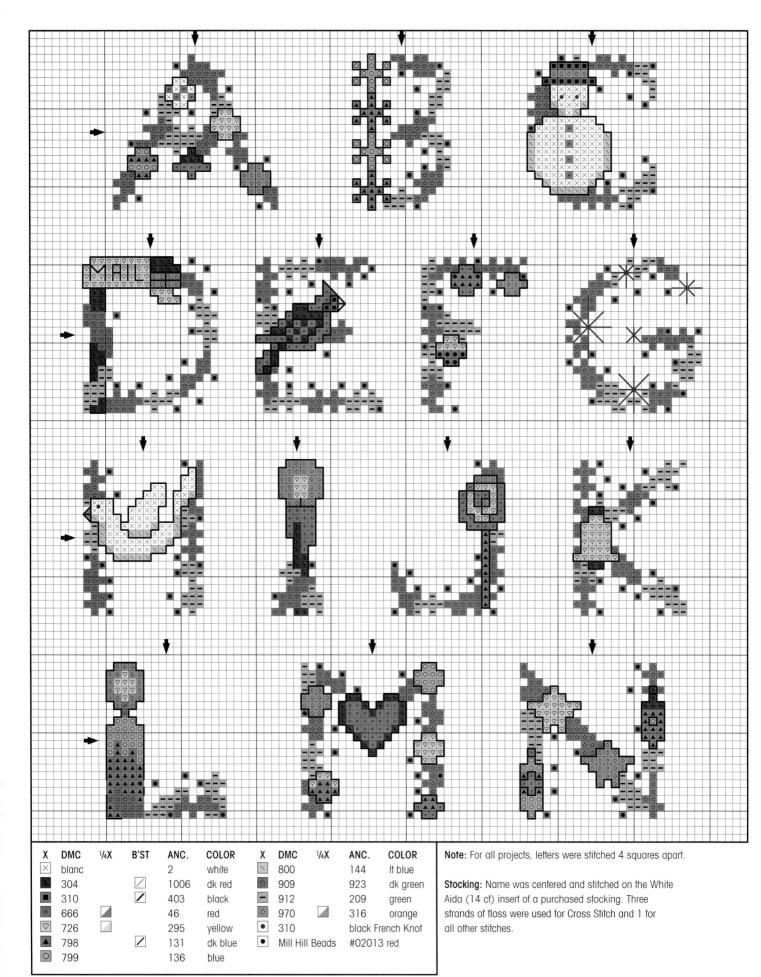

X	DMC	¼X	B'ST	ANC.	COLOR
☒	blanc			2	white
◨	304	◸		1006	dk red
■	310	◿		403	black
✳	666	◺		46	red
♡	726	◺		295	yellow
▲	798	◿		131	dk blue
◉	799			136	blue

X	DMC	¼X	ANC.	COLOR
◩	800		144	lt blue
✶	909		923	dk green
▬	912		209	green
◇	970	◿	316	orange
●	310			black French Knot
⬤	Mill Hill Beads		#02013 red

Note: For all projects, letters were stitched 4 squares apart.

Stocking: Name was centered and stitched on the White Aida (14 ct) insert of a purchased stocking. Three strands of floss were used for Cross Stitch and 1 for all other stitches.

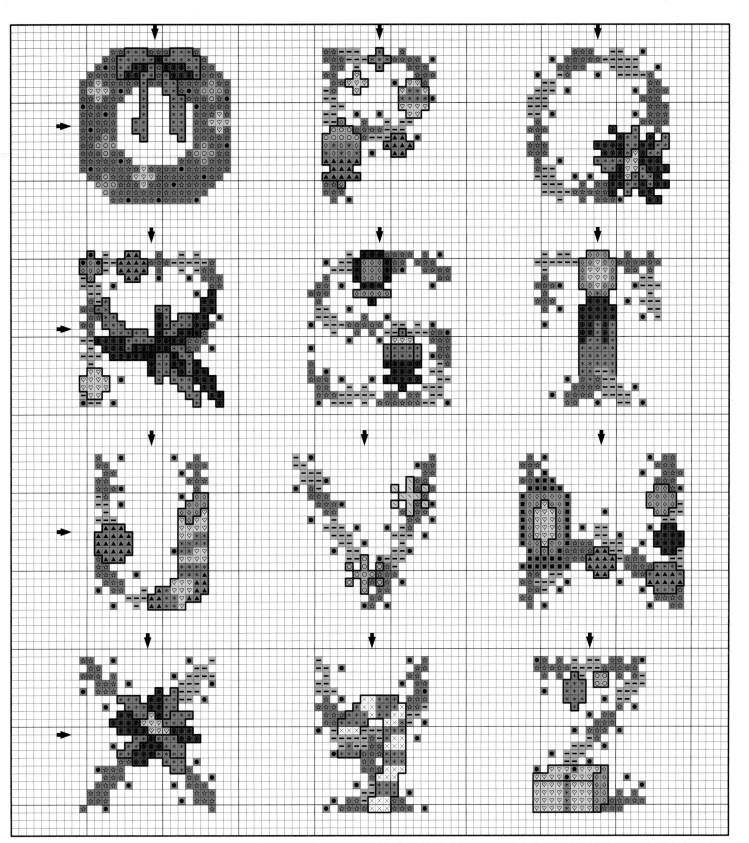

Sweater: "JOY" was stitched over an 8" x 6" piece of 14 mesh waste canvas on a White Bearly Sweater. Three strands of floss were used for Cross Stitch and 1 for all other stitches. See Using Waste Canvas, pg.143.

Sweatshirt: "CHEERS" was stitched over a 16" x 6" piece of 11 mesh waste canvas on a purchased sweatshirt.

Six strands of floss were used for Cross Stitch, 2 for Backstitch, and 3 for French Knots. See Using Waste Canvas, pg. 143.

Towel: "NOEL" was centered and stitched on the White Aida (14 ct) insert of a prefinished towel. Three strands of floss were used for Cross Stitch and 1 for all other stitches.

Mini Pillows: "C" and "M" were each stitched on a 7" square of White Aida (14 ct). Three strands of floss were used for Cross Stitch and 1 for all other stitches. See Fringed Pillow Ornament, pg. 143.

Design by Barbara Christopher.

139

Whimsical Accents

Whether they're frolicking on the tree as ornaments or adding whimsy to an afghan, this trio of designs will delight anyone on your gift list. Aren't they precious!

X	DMC	¼ X	B'ST	ANC.	COLOR
☆	blanc	☆		2	white
Σ	ecru			387	ecru
■	310		✓	403	black
✳	321			9046	red
◎	353			6	dk flesh
◖	367			217	green
▲	434			310	dk brown
◉	435			1046	brown
C	436			1045	lt brown
d	437			362	vy lt brown
✦	498			1005	dk red
▽	645			273	grey
▽	666			46	lt red
Π	725			305	yellow
★	738			361	tan
□	739			387	lt tan
‖	754			1012	flesh
✕	762			234	lt grey
T	844			1041	dk grey
+	931			1034	blue
✔	948			1011	lt flesh
4	3072			847	vy lt grey
◉	blanc			2	white Fr. Knot
●	310			403	black Fr. Knot

Designs were stitched on White Aida (18 ct). Two strands of floss were used for Cross Stitch and 1 for Backstitch and French Knots. They were inserted in round gold frames (2¹/₂" dia. opening). Designs were also stitched on a White All-Cotton Anne Cloth (18 ct) afghan over two fabric threads. Six strands of floss were used for Cross Stitch and 2 for Backstitch and French Knots. See Afghan Diagram for placement of designs. See Afghan Preparation, pg. 143.

Designs by Pat Olson.

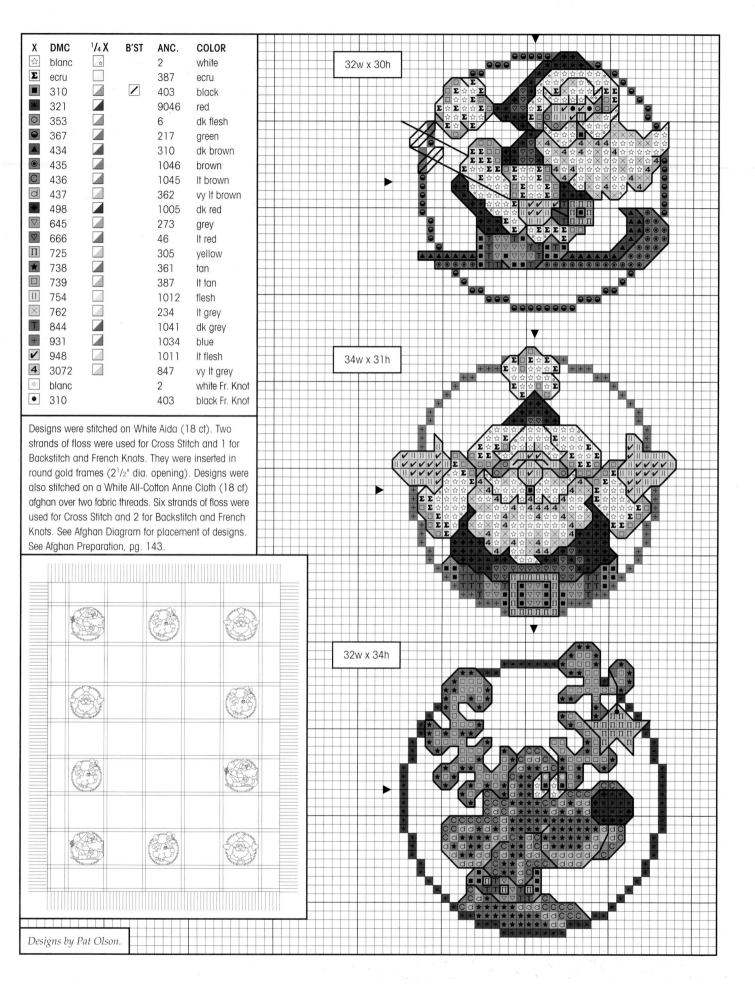

32w x 30h

34w x 31h

32w x 34h

How to Read Charts

Each chart is made up of a key and a gridded design where each square represents a stitch. The symbols in the key tell which floss color to use for each stitch in the chart. The following headings and symbols are given:

X — Cross Stitch
DMC — DMC color number
¼ X — One-Quarter Stitch
¾ X — Three-Quarter Stitch
B'ST — Backstitch
ANC. — Anchor color number
COLOR — the name given to the floss color in this chart

A square filled with a color and a symbol should be worked as a **Cross Stitch**.

A triangle (with or without a symbol) should be worked as a **One-Quarter Stitch** or a **Three-Quarter Stitch**.

A straight line should be worked as a **Backstitch**.

A large dot listed near the end of the key should be worked as a **French Knot**.

In the chart, the symbol for a **Cross Stitch** may be omitted, reduced, or partially covered when a **Backstitch** crosses its square. Refer to the background color to determine the floss color.

How to Stitch

Always work **Cross Stitches**, **One-Quarter Stitches**, and **Three-Quarter Stitches** first and then add the **Backstitch** and **French Knots**.

Cross Stitch (X): For horizontal rows, work stitches in two journeys (*Fig. 1*). For vertical rows, complete each stitch as shown (*Fig. 2*). When working over two fabric threads, work Cross Stitch as shown in **Fig. 3**.

Fig. 1

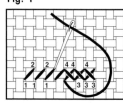

Fig. 2

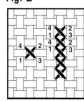

Fig. 3

Quarter Stitch (¼X and ¾X): Stitch 1-2 is the One-Quarter Stitch (¼X) (*Fig. 4*). When stitches 1-4 are worked in the same color, the resulting stitch is called a Three-Quarter Stitch (¾X). **Fig. 5** shows this technique when working over two fabric threads.

Fig. 4

Fig. 5

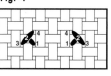

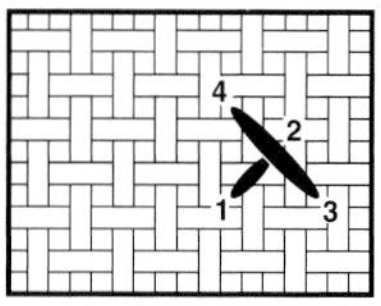

Backstitch (B'ST): For outlines and details, Backstitch should be worked after the design has been completed (*Fig. 6*). When working over two fabric threads, work Backstitch as shown in **Fig. 7**.

Fig. 6

Fig. 7

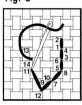

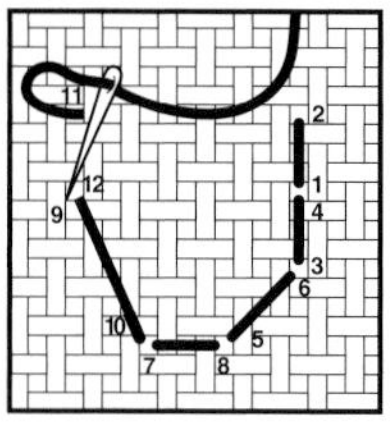

French Knot: Bring needle up at 1. Wrap floss once around needle. Insert needle at 2, tighten knot, and pull needle through fabric, holding floss until it must be released (*Fig. 8*). For a larger knot, use more floss strands; wrap only once.

Fig. 8

Running Stitch: Work Running Stitch as shown in **Fig. 9** stitching over and under desired number of fabric threads.

Fig. 9

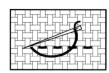

Attaching Beads

To sew beads in place, use floss and a fine needle that will pass through beads. Secure floss on back of fabric. Bring needle up where indicated on chart, then run needle through one bead and down through fabric (*Fig. 10*). Secure floss on back or move to next bead.

Fig. 10

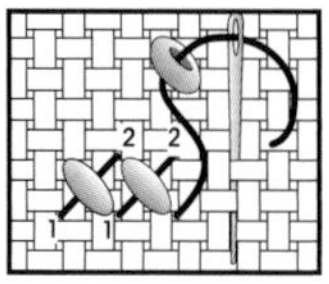

Stitching Tips

Preparing Fabric

Being sure to allow plenty of margin, cut fabric desired size and overcast raw edges. It is better to waste a little fabric than to come up short after hours of stitching!

Working with Floss

To ensure smoother stitches, separate strands and realign them before threading needle. Keep stitching tension consistent. Begin and end floss by running under several stitches on back; never tie knots.

Dye Lot Variation

It is important to buy all of the floss you need to complete your project from the same dye lot. Although variations in color may be slight when flosses from two different dye lots are held together, the variation is usually apparent on a stitched piece.

Where to Start

The horizontal and vertical centers of each charted design are shown by arrows. You may start at any point on the charted design, but be sure the design will be centered on the fabric. Locate the center of fabric by folding in half, top to bottom and again left to right. On the charted design, count the number of squares (stitches) from the center of the chart to where you wish to start. Then from the fabric's center, find your starting point by counting out the same number of fabric threads (stitches). (*To work over two fabric threads, count out twice the number of fabric threads.*)

Working over Two Fabric Threads

When working over two fabric threads, the stitches should be placed so that vertical fabric threads support each stitch. Make sure that the first Cross Stitch is placed on the fabric with stitch 1-2 beginning and ending where a vertical fabric thread crosses over a horizontal fabric thread (*Fig. 11*).

Fig. 11

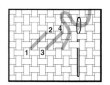

Cutting Perforated Plastic

When cutting perforated plastic, make sure to cut as close to the thread as possible without cutting into the thread. A craft knife is helpful when cutting a small area from the center of a larger piece of plastic. When using a craft knife, protect the table below your plastic with a layer of cardboard or a magazine.

Using Perforated Paper

Perforated paper has a right side and a wrong side. The right side is smoother and stitching should be done on this side. Do not fold paper. To locate center of paper, use a ruler to measure width and height of paper; then mark lightly with a pencil at center of these measurements. Find the square where the lines intersect and mark center lightly. Perforated paper will tear if handled roughly; therefore, hold paper flat while stitching and do not use a hoop. Use the stab method when stitching. Carry floss across back as little as possible; thread pulled too tightly may tear the paper. After stitching, carefully erase visible pencil marks.

Using Vinyl-Weave™

Hold Vinyl-Weave™ flat while stitching and do not use a hoop. Stitch using a #7 sharp needle. Quarter stitches may be stitched by splitting the vinyl with the needle.

Using Waste Canvas

Cut canvas 2" larger than design; cover edges with masking tape. Cut a piece of lightweight, non-fusible interfacing same size as canvas to provide a firm stitching base. Baste canvas and interfacing to garment. Place garment in hoop; work design using a sharp needle. Trim canvas to within $3/4$" of design. Dampen canvas slightly to remove sizing. Use tweezers to pull out canvas threads one at a time.

Afghan Preparation

Cut off selvages. Fabric should measure 45"w x 58"l. Measure $5 1/2$" from raw edge of fabric and pull out one fabric thread. Fringe fabric up to missing thread. Repeat for each side. Tie an overhand knot at each corner with 4 horizontal and 4 vertical fabric threads. Working from corners, use 8 fabric threads for each knot until all threads are knotted.

Project Finishing

Bordered Pillow Ornaments

When sewing, match right sides and raw edges and use a $1/2$" seam allowance unless noted.

Trim stitched piece to desired finished size plus $1/2$" on all sides.

Cut two $1 1/4$" wide fabric strips the same length as one side edge of stitched piece. Sew strips to side edges of stitched piece. Cut two $1 1/4$" wide fabric strips the same length as top edge of stitched piece and attached strips. Sew strips to top and bottom edges of stitched piece. Cut one piece of backing fabric same size as front. Sew front to back, leaving an opening for turning. Trim corners diagonally, turn right side out, and press. Stuff with polyester fiberfill; slipstitch opening closed. For hanger, fold and sew an 8" length of ribbon to back of pillow. Tack a jingle bell to top of pillow.

Corded Pillow Ornament

When sewing, match right sides and raw edges and use a $1/2$" seam allowance unless noted.

Trim stitched piece to desired finished size plus $1/2$" on all sides for seam allowances. Cut backing fabric same size as stitched piece. Sew stitched piece and backing fabric together, leaving an opening for turning. Clip seam allowances at corners. Turn ornament right side out and stuff with polyester fiberfill; slipstitch opening closed.

For twisted cording, measure around ornament. Add any length needed for hanger; add another 5". Multiply by 3. Cut 6 pieces each of two or three colors of floss this length. (*If using metallic floss, cut four strands the determined length to use with the other floss colors.*) Aligning floss ends, tie an overhand knot at each end. Holding one knot in one hand, hook remaining knot over a drawer knob and pull taut. Keeping floss pulled taut, twist clockwise until floss begins to twist back on itself. Hold floss at midpoint with free hand, then fold knotted end to meet end at knob and hold ends together. Let midpoint go to allow floss to twist. Knot floss ends together at knob and cut twisted cording from knob. Pull twisted cording between fingers to smooth. Attach cording to ornament.

Mini Tote Ornament

When sewing, match right sides and raw edges and use a $1/2$" seam allowance.

For tote front, trim stitched piece to $7 1/2$"w x 7"h with top of design $1 3/4$" from top edge. For tote back, cut a piece of fabric $7 1/2$"w x 7"h. Match tote front and back; sew sides and bottom together. Trim bottom corner seam allowances diagonally and press seam allowances open. To form bottom corners, place right sides together and match side seams to bottom seam; sew across each corner 1" from end. Turn right side out. For handles, cut two 9" lengths of $5/8$"w ribbon. To place handles on tote front, measure in $1 1/4$" from each side seam and mark with a pin. Matching raw edges, pin ends of one handle to right side of tote front at placement marks. (*Make sure handle is not twisted.*) Repeat to pin second handle to tote back. Sew handles to tote body $1/4$" from raw edges. Press top edge of tote body $1/4$" to wrong side. Press $1/4$" to wrong side again. With handles extending above top of tote, sew around top through all thicknesses.

Paper-Backed Ornaments

Glue stitched piece to white paper. Trim perforated plastic and paper to 1 square from design. Glue to colored paper. Use decorative-edge scissors to trim paper to $1/8$".

Fringed Pillow Ornament

With design centered on fabric, cut stitched piece and backing fabric (same fabric as stitched piece) desired width and height plus $1/2$" on all four sides to allow for fringe. Matching wrong sides and raw edges, use desired floss color to cross stitch fabric pieces together $1/2$" from bottom and side edges. Stuff pillow with polyester fiberfill; cross stitch across top of pillow $1/2$" from edges. Fringe fabric to one square from cross-stitched lines. If desired, tack ribbon to pillow for hanger.

Stiffened Accessory

For backing, cut a piece of cotton fabric same size as stitched piece. Apply a coat of fabric stiffener to back of stitched piece. Matching wrong sides, place backing on stitched piece; allow to dry. Apply another coat of stiffener to backing; allow to dry. Trim stiffened piece to desired size.

Padded Shape Ornament #1

Trace appropriate ornament pattern (pg. 145) onto tracing paper; cut out. Draw around pattern twice on lightweight cardboard and twice on batting; cut out. Place one piece of batting on each cardboard piece. Center pattern over stitched piece; cut stitched piece $1/2$" larger than pattern. Cut backing fabric same size as stitched piece. Center stitched piece right side up on batting; fold and glue edges to back of cardboard, clipping fabric as necessary. Repeat with backing fabric and remaining cardboard piece for ornament back. For cording, cut a 2" wide bias strip of fabric the same measurement as outer edge of ornament plus 3". Center $1/4$" diameter cord on wrong side of bias strip. Matching long raw edges, fold bias strip over cord. Using a zipper foot and gently stretching fabric as you sew, baste next to cord. Trim seam allowances to $1/2$".

Beginning at center bottom, pin cording to back of ornament front along outer edge, clipping seam allowances as necessary to allow cording to lie flat. Beginning and ending 2" from each end of cording, glue cording to back of ornament front along outer edge. Cut off one end of cording so it overlaps the other end by 1". Remove 2" of stitching from loose end of cording. Cut cord so ends butt together. Fold loose end of bias strip under $1/2$"; lap it around other end. Continue to glue cording to back of ornament front. For hanger, glue folded $1/4$"w ribbon to wrong side of ornament front. Glue wrong sides of ornament front and back together. Weight with a heavy book until glue is dry.

Padded Shape Ornament #2

For pattern, use tracing paper and draw around stitched piece close to edge of design; cut out pattern. Draw around pattern twice on lightweight cardboard and twice on batting; cut out. Glue one piece of batting on each cardboard piece.

Center pattern over stitched piece; cut stitched piece $1/2$" larger than pattern. Cut backing fabric same size as stitched piece. Center stitched piece right side up on batting; fold and glue edges to back of cardboard, clipping fabric as necessary. Repeat with backing fabric and remaining cardboard piece for ornament back.

For cording, cut a length of $1/4$" dia. purchased cording (with seam allowance) the same measurement as outer edge of ornament plus 1". Beginning and ending at bottom center of stitched piece, glue cording seam allowance to wrong side of ornament front, overlapping ends of cording. Matching wrong sides, glue ornament front and back together.

Bag Ornaments

Cut a piece of fabric 6"w x 19"l. Center and stitch design with top of design 2" from one end. Fold fabric in half with wrong sides together. Beginning 4 squares from design, use embroidery floss to work Running Stitch (over and under 2 threads) along each side through both thicknesses. Cut a 10" length of $1/8$"w ribbon. Beginning at center front $1 1/4$" from top edge, work Running Stitch around front and back of ornament. Fringe all raw edges to within 3 squares from Running Stitch. Place cinnamon sticks in ornament; pull ribbon ends to gather ribbon around cinnamon sticks. Tie ribbon in a bow and trim ends. For hanger, fold an 8" length of $1/8$"w ribbon in half and tack ends to gathering line at center back of ornament.

Fabric-Backed Ornaments

Trace appropriate ornament pattern (pg. 145) onto tracing paper; cut out pattern. Cut one piece of paper-backed fusible web the same size as stitched piece. Matching edges, follow manufacturer's instructions to fuse web to wrong side of stitched piece. Center and pin pattern on top of stitched piece; cut out and remove pattern. Remove paper backing from fusible web. Refer to photo to use two strands of a coordinating floss color to randomly sew running stitch $1/8$" from edge of stitched piece. Center and fuse wrong side of stitched piece to right side of a 5" square of fabric. Use pinking shears to cut fabric $1/4$" larger than stitched piece. For hanger, fold and glue a 6" piece of rickrack to back of ornament.

Corded Hanging Pillow

When making pillow, always match right sides and raw edges and use a $1/2$" seam allowance.
Trim stitched piece to desired finished size plus $1/2$" on all sides for seam allowances. Cut a piece of fabric the same size as stitched piece for backing. For cording, cut one length of $1/4$" diameter cord same measurement as outer edge of pillow front plus 5". For cording fabric, cut one 2"w bias fabric strip same length as cord. For hanger, cut two 15" lengths of $1/8$"w ribbon.

Center cord on wrong side of cording fabric. Matching long edges, fold cording fabric over cord. Gently stretching fabric as you sew, use zipper foot to baste next to cord. Beginning 1" from one end, baste cording to pillow front, clipping seam allowances at corners to allow cording to lie flat. Leaving needle in fabric, cut off one end of cording so it overlaps the other end by 1". Remove 1" of stitching from loose end of cording. Holding fabric away from cord, cut cord so ends butt together. Fold loose end of fabric under $1/2$", lap it around other end, and continue stitching cording to pillow front. Sew stitched piece and backing fabric together, leaving an opening for turning. Trim corners diagonally, turn right side out, and press. Stuff pillow with polyester fiberfill and slipstitch opening closed. For hanger, slipstitch ribbon ends to back of pillow. Tie free ends in a bow.

Ruffled Pillow

When making pillow, always match right sides and raw edges and use a $1/2$" seam allowance.
Trim stitched piece to desired finished size plus $1/4$" on all sides.
Cut one piece of fabric desired finished size plus $1/2$" on all sides for seam allowances. Center and baste stitched piece to pillow front. Cut a length of purchased trim the outer measurement of stitched piece plus 1". Sew trim to pillow front, covering raw edges of stitched piece and overlapping beginning end. Cut one fabric strip two times the desired finished width plus 1" for seam allowances and two times the measurement of outer edge of pillow front. Sew ends of ruffle together; press seam open. With wrong sides together, press ruffle in half. To gather ruffle, baste $3/8$" and $1/4$" from raw edge. Pull basting threads, gathering ruffle to fit edge of pillow front. Baste ruffle to pillow front.
Cut one piece of backing fabric same size as pillow front. Sew front to back, leaving an opening for turning. Trim corners diagonally, turn right side out, and press. Stuff pillow with polyester fiberfill; slipstitch opening closed.

Jar Lid

Mason jar puff-up kits may be purchased for both regular and wide mouth jar lids; mounting instructions are included in kit. If a kit is not available, a padded mounting board can be made. Using flat piece of lid for pattern, cut a circle from adhesive mounting board. Using opening of screw ring for pattern, cut a circle of batting. Center batting on adhesive side of board; press into place. Center stitched piece on board and press edges onto adhesive. Trim edges close to board. Glue board inside screw ring.

Mug

Beginning 1" from desired short edge, stitch design on a $10 1/4$"w x $3 1/2$"h piece of Vinyl-Weave™ (14 ct) using a #7 sharp needle. *(Stitch design at right end of vinyl if mug is to be used by a right-handed person and at left end of vinyl for a left-handed person.)* Place Vinyl-Weave™ in a Stitch-A-Mug™ with short ends of vinyl aligned with handle. Remove stitched piece before washing mug.

Some cover items made by Pat Johnson, Donna Overman, Angie Perryman, Anne Simpson, and Helen Stanton.